Lyndsay Green is a pioneering sociologist and
researcher who spent her career helping people
use communications technologies for learning.
After raising two children who never knew a time
before computers, she has turned her knowledge
of new technologies to providing parents with the
tools they need for bringing up teens in an online
world. Green is a highly sought-after speaker and
moderator at national and international organizations. The American textbook *Computers and
Information Systems* calls Green an "information
agent of the future."

Books of Merit

Teens Gone Wired:
Are You Ready?

Teens Gone Wired: Are You Ready?

Lyndsay Green

THOMAS ALLEN PUBLISHERS

TORONTO

Library and Archives Canada Cataloguing in Publication

Green, Lyndsay
    Teens gone wired : are you ready? / Lyndsay Green.

Includes bibliographical references.
ISBN 978-0-88762-809-2

1. Parent and teenager.   2. Technology and youth.
3. Internet and teenagers.   4. Teenagers—Conduct of life.
5. Parenting.   6. Information technology—Moral and ethical aspects.   I. Title.

HQ799.15.G74   2011   649'.125   C2011-903585-5

Editors: Katherine Ashenburg and Patrick Crean
Cover design: Sputnik Design Partners Inc.
Cover image: Getty Images

Published by Thomas Allen Publishers,
a division of Thomas Allen & Son Limited,
390 Steelcase Road East,
Markham, Ontario L3R 1G2 Canada

www.thomasallen.ca

The publisher gratefully acknowledges the support of The Ontario Arts
Council for its publishing program.

We acknowledge the support of the Canada Council for the Arts, which last
year invested $20.1 million in writing and publishing throughout Canada.

We acknowledge the Government of Ontario through the Ontario Media
Development Corporation's Ontario Book Initiative.

We acknowledge the financial support of the Government of Canada
through the Canada Book Fund for our publishing activities.

1 2 3 4 5   15 14 13 12 11

Text printed on a 100% PCW recycled stock

Printed and bound in Canada

This book is dedicated to my husband who is my steadfast co-parent and to our two (former) teens who are living proof of the theory of evolution.

Acknowledgements

This book would not exist without the generosity and wisdom of the contributors who shared their stories with me. I am extraordinarily blessed that the following parents, teens and former teens were willing to contribute their insights and advice: Sylvia Bashevkin, Linda Black, Rita Bode, Susan Carter, Alastair Cheng, Sanjay Cishecki, Suzie Cunningham, Mallory Davenport, Pamela Earle, Charles Feaver, Barb Fritz, Anne Godfrey, Liz Gordon, Kristin Grant, Robbie Grant, Rory Grant, Patricia Hanrahan, Karen Hersey, Janine Hunt, Kathleen Hunt, Laurie Intven, Natalie Intven, Tess Intven, Bill Kurchak, Karen Laing, Zach Loader, Sue Matcuk Maden, Bella Manu, Sasha Manu, Clare Marshall, Maureen Matthews, Katherine McAuley, Martha McGloin, Barbara McIssac, Marylou Miers, Marie Morgan, Catherine Murray, Lily Nolan, Joanna Patrick, Doris Penner, Bob Presner, Rohini Ramanathan, Edye Rome, Gabriela Schonbach, Anni Shi, Melanie Smith, Anne Taylor, Grace Westcott and Sheila Williams. The book benefitted greatly from the feedback I received to earlier drafts from the following people who applied their professional expertise and/or parental experience to improving the book and enhancing its value: Maureen Brown, Vince Gilpin, Ainslie Gray, Shari Graydon, Laurie Intven, Joanna Patrick, Sue Matcuk Maden, Bella Manu, Marcia McClung, Maureen McEvoy, Jim Oldford, Suzanne Robinson, Henry Rose, Melanie Smith and Grace Westcott. A special thanks to my former professor Barry Wellman who continues to mentor me and reminds me that "not everything that counts can be counted and not everything that can be counted counts, but some things should be counted." My heartfelt thanks to my editors Katherine Ashenburg and Patrick Crean, the dream team who pushed me to make the book the best it could be, and to my agent, Beverley Slopen, who is out there advocating on my behalf. My deepest thanks are reserved for my husband and our two daughters whose life experiences inspired this book and who collaborated with open hearts to lay bare the teen years. The exuberance with which they embrace life inspires me daily.

Contents

The Teen-Parent Connection   205

Conclusion   257

Websites for Parents   261

Notes   269

Teens Gone Wired: Are You Ready?

Background

S HE's only fourteen years old and her life is ruined," said my friend Rennie. "She'll never be able to erase that image, and it will haunt her forever." Rennie was talking about an acquaintance who had been engaging in sexual activity with a fellow student when another student captured the event on a cellphone. The photo had been posted online. Rennie and I talked about the young woman, as well as the other actors in this drama: the young man who had participated, the photographer, the person who uploaded the image, and those who were circulating it. Rennie, who has four children, the eldest of whom is thirteen, summed up her feelings: "I feel really unlucky to be parenting teens in this day and age."

It's easy to understand Rennie's anxieties. We're inundated with horror stories involving teens and the online world. An eighteen-year-old Rutgers University freshman commits suicide after his sexual encounter with another young man is videotaped by his roommate and posted on the Internet.[1] In a small town in British Columbia, a drugged sixteen-year-old girl is gang-raped and a sixteen-year-old boy circulates images of the atrocity online. And then there is Ashleigh Hall, the seventeen-year-old British student who was kidnapped, raped and murdered by a convicted sex offender who ensnared her by using a fake Facebook profile in which he pretended to be a teenage boy.[2]

In addition to these blatant dangers, there are subtler problems lurking in cyberspace that could profoundly affect our teens. Some people believe that the incessant demands of digital multi-tasking may be rendering them incapable of thinking profoundly or focusing deeply. Exposure to pornography may be distorting their understanding of healthy sexuality, and vivid images of gratuitous violence may be desensitizing them and reducing their ability to empathize. Opportunities to post every detail of their lives on social-networking sites such as Facebook and Twitter may be turning them into narcissistic, self-absorbed individuals with a sense of entitlement.

At the same time, we know that our children's futures will depend on their ability to exploit the benefits of the digital world skillfully and turn it to their advantage. And we know their lives will increasingly be lived in cyberspace, whether we like it or not. So we need to give our children the skills to maximize the potential of the digital world while simultaneously mediating its downsides, and we need to keep them safe. All this can seem like a tall order. Our teenagers' world—with its social networking, webcams, interactive games and constant texting—can be pretty intimidating, and it's easy to feel we lack the expertise to parent effectively. I wrote this book for my friend Rennie and for all parents who are anticipating the teen years with dread. By providing you with practical tips, resources and strategies, I hope to prepare you for the challenges we face raising teens today. At the same time, I want to emphasize the flip side and show you how this same online world can support us in parenting our teens. Along the way, I'm hoping to change Rennie's mind, and yours too. Contrary to Rennie's conclusion that her timing was unlucky, I want to convince you that we are fortunate to be parenting in these times.

There is a practical reason for our good fortune. Never before have parents had so many resources at our fingertips, such a wealth of valuable material that can be instantly accessed online to support us in parenting our teens. And never before have teens themselves had access to so many resources designed for and often by them, to help them face their challenges. This book provides links to websites on everything from eating disorders, to sexual identity, to money management. There are medically supported websites that can help you learn about the signs of depression, understand substance abuse, or figure out what puberty is doing to your teen's body. And many websites have separate sections, designed and resourced differently for parents and teenagers. Also, there are websites that suggest solutions for the very problems generated by the Internet itself.

For all the criticisms that are thrown at the online world and the negative things it is doing to our children (and to us), there are impressive positive sides. While the Internet has the potential to isolate our teenagers, it can also extend their community. Cyberspace could encourage them to become self-absorbed narcissists, but it can also help them become caring citizens of the world. Living online could potentially turn them into shallow thinkers, but it can also help them problem-solve and multi-task.

My optimism is grounded in a long-standing relationship with computers that began when I was barely out of my teens and my job as a research assistant required inputting data cards into our university's mainframe computer. Over the next four decades, as new hardware and software were introduced at a dizzying pace, I spent my career helping adults use technology for learning. It was in 1984, just months before my first daughter was born, that I bought my first computer. That decision was life-changing and allowed me to combine childrearing and work in a way that would have been previously impossible.

My two daughters, now in their twenties, have never known a day without computers. I taught them about computers so they would be skilled in their use, but it was our relationship with the technology that contained the more important lesson. I tried to impress upon them the need to make the digital world our slave, rather than letting it enslave us. My "selfish cellphone" is a good example. I owned one of the very early cellphones but never gave out the number, saying it was only for outgoing calls. People were frustrated that I could call them and interrupt their lives, but they couldn't do the same to me. Now, decades later, my iPhone could run my life with its incessant texts, e-mails, Twitter feeds and calls, but I do my best to stay in charge. And the same goes for our home. People have called our house "old-fashioned" because the room where we spend most of our time has no technology, apart from a stereo, and, at our parties, people are actively discouraged from pulling out cellphones. They say that for someone whose career has been spent with technology it's surprising the way I restrict its use. That is the lesson I have tried to pass on to my daughters.

But as technology casts its web over more and more of our lives, it is becoming harder and harder to ensure that we are using technology, rather than being used by it. This may be especially true for our teens, who have known no life other than an online one. But we adults, too, are struggling to understand how to harness technology to sustain us rather than swallowing us whole. When we remind our teens of the downsides of living completely in the virtual world, or of the risks of neglecting real friends for online relationships, or of the rudeness of interrupting face-to-face conversations to connect in cyberspace, we are confronting our own struggles. And while we need to guide our teens through new problems, such as online bullying and cyberstalking that are unique to the digital world, we are discovering that issues from our own teen years, like sex, drugs and drinking, are imbedded in a new landscape. Problems may surface in new guises, but underneath they're often the perennial issues teens have always faced as they navigate their way to maturity. My hope is that the advice in this book will help you parent with vigilance and with knowledge, but also with a profound self-awareness. And I hope that being forewarned and forearmed will allow you to have more fun while parenting your teens in an online world.

Introduction

THIS BOOK is woven around stories—the kind we tell one another while sitting around the kitchen table or at the sports arena. They are gathered from three dozen mothers and fathers, and a dozen young people. Because the parents told me stories that belonged not just to them, but also to their teenagers, and because the teenagers are teenagers, I have changed everyone's names. Protecting their privacy gave the contributors the freedom to be candid, and their stories have an honesty that reveals hard-won insights. My own two daughters have been afforded some measure of privacy by remaining nameless. In this way, as one of them joked, "Now it looks like you have just one horribly messed-up kid."

The book has been greatly enriched by more than a dozen experts: doctors, psychologists, educators and therapists who reviewed the manuscript, suggested additional resources and kept me from straying into areas where I lack expertise. I thank them for their guidance. And while I say this book is about *teenagers*, the young people we talk about cover the spectrum of puberty, from boys and girls as young as ten and eleven up to young men and women in their early twenties. Being a teenager is more a state of mind and body than a number.

Because issues involving our teens are rarely clear-cut, I've structured the book as a series of fine lines. Throughout the teen years it's often hard to differentiate between good and bad, healthy and unhealthy, normal and aberrant, and the demarcation seems to shift daily. When our children are online are they wasting their time or acquiring essential job skills? Are they becoming superb multi-taskers or losing their ability to focus? Are they experimenting or crossing the line? Are they just having fun or are they addicted? And then there is the health and well-being of our teens, which sometimes appears to change overnight. Is your teen in great physical shape or does he have an eating disorder? Is your daughter clinically depressed or just having a down day? Is it preferable that your teen is drinking rather than taking drugs, or is he becoming an alcoholic? And if you think the lines are clearly drawn, then the arguments you read in this book may blur them. My hope is that the book's stories and resources will help you clarify these distinctions when it comes to your own teenager.

Emphasizing life's fine lines was a parenting strategy my husband and I used with our children. We debated issues with them from a very young age, and one friend remembers being shocked to witness my daughters discussing the pros and cons of euthanasia when they were not much beyond diapers. We wanted them to understand that the world is not black and white, and that it is the shades of grey that make life so rich. It is these nuances that make decision making so complicated, problem solving so exciting, and policy making so challenging. The problem with our approach is that by the time our daughters reached their teen years they had become very effective debaters. And if we didn't see how there could possibly be any fine lines in a particular situation, they were quick to point them out.

Parenting a teen often feels like walking a tightrope in a high-wire act—another very fine line. You can be carefully discussing something with your child, pursuing a line of reasoning that seems to be fruitful and well accepted, when suddenly you make a misstep, you lose your footing, they stomp away, and the moment is lost. Or, seemingly overnight, your sunny child becomes an angry, petulant stranger and it seems that some invisible line has been crossed, and you're wondering what happened. One day, you're doing something seemingly unremarkable—using your child's nickname, tousling his hair, wearing a certain outfit—and, without warning, you've crossed the line from acceptability to affront.

Fine lines will be our constant companion as we parent our teens in an online world, and developing our parenting strategies will be an exercise in figuring out where the line should be drawn. In the following sections, I've grouped the fine lines under the categories of the teen mind, the social teen, the teen spirit, the teen citizen, the teen body and the teen-parent connection.

The Teen Mind

Practising for Life vs. Wasting Time

ONE of our constant complaints about teens today is the countless hours they spend connected to some form of digital device. It's not just our imagination. Indeed, they *are* plugged in a lot of the time. Current estimates are that children aged eight to eighteen spend more than seven and a half hours per day in digital activity of one form or another, and that doesn't include cellphone use.[1] Here's what they are doing: using some form of social-networking platform such as Facebook or MySpace, playing online games, posting and/or watching videos on YouTube, using e-mail or some form of instant messaging, and, maybe, they are doing their homework. They are using cellphones mainly for texting, with a third of them sending more than one hundred messages daily. Most teens don't have a smartphone (e.g., BlackBerry or iPhone) yet but might be angling for one. They aren't particularly interested in Twitter, but that might change.[2]

They are increasingly accessing the online world through a wireless connection, which means there are few places where they can't be connected. And, even before I've finished writing this sentence, they will be using new platforms, new software and new functions.

Contemplating all those hours spent in cyberspace, we worry that our teens are letting their lives drain through their fingertips and wonder whether we should be intervening. What your teen is doing is walking one of those fine lines between wasting her time and practising for life. And, yes, there are times we should intervene. The Center for Internet Addiction Recovery (see p. 261 for the URL) has developed a test to help us assess whether our teen is dealing with an addiction to the Internet. Here are some questions to ponder: "How often does he seem withdrawn from others since discovering the Internet?"; "How often does she become defensive or secretive when asked what she does on-line?"; "How often do his grades suffer because of the amount of time he spends on-line?"; "How often does she seem preoccupied with being back on-line when off-line?"

Yes, there are potential problems. But we need to acknowledge that, unless our teen decides to withdraw from the world, a good portion of her adult life will probably be lived online, and her career success will likely depend on acquiring a great deal of skill with digital tools. Already the working lives of many adults are lived as much in the online as the face-to-face world. We telecommute, participate in online meetings, post on internal Wikis, maintain team blogs, create websites, access training online and create avatars to attend conferences held in virtual-reality sites such as Second Life. The workplaces that our teens will be entering will require even higher levels of digital competency.

So, our job as parents is to help our teens mitigate the downsides of the online world while reaping the benefits. Dr. Kimberly Young, a psychologist who founded the Center for Internet Addiction Recovery, compares Internet dependency to an eating disorder. "Technology, like food, is an essential part of daily life, and those suffering from disordered online behaviour cannot give it up entirely and instead have to learn moderation and controlled use."[3] We need a combination of strategies, both monitoring and education, to help our teens learn to control their online behaviour.

Let's take my young friend Sean as an example. By age eleven, Sean was making PowerPoint presentations for school assignments and using them to lobby his parents for stuff he wanted—a cellphone, increases in allowance or later bedtimes. Through the Internet he learned how to use Photoshop and GarageBand where he composes music, Word and Excel where he makes charts and diagrams for homework, iMovie where he edits films for school assignments and YouTube where he posts videos. By age thirteen, his cellphone was replaced with an iPhone, and by age fourteen he had his own computer. Now, at fifteen, most of his homework is done on the computer. He uses the Internet for research and for social networking through Facebook, which has all but replaced e-mail for him and his friends. He stays in touch with friends through calls and texting on his iPhone. Texting is also his preferred mode of communicating with his parents. He has accumulated a large number of apps (applications) for his iPhone, some of which are informative, like the weather and local transit schedules, while others explore subjects of interest, like space. Many others are games.

Sean's parents are somewhat worried about the amount of time he spends on the computer. Most weekdays when he comes home from school, he heads straight to his computer to check Facebook. After dinner, he disappears into his room and spends the evening on his computer doing a combination of things, including homework. He watches TV shows on his computer for the convenience of watching what he wants when he wants. His parents have decided not to place restrictions on his computer use. They feel that at age fifteen he is entitled to his privacy and the freedom to make choices, to think about their consequences and to make adjustments. They remind themselves that Sean is doing well at school, shows no signs of behavioural problems and remains actively involved in his karate, rugby and guitar.

"These are all positive signs that Sean is managing well," says his mother, "and that his computer has not swallowed him up. I do believe that less time on the computer would free up time for him to spend on other things. I make sure that I occasionally remind him of this and try to entice him with other opportunities, but ultimately the amount of use will remain his decision—as long as everything else continues to go well."

But what if your teen is spending too much time online and is not doing well at school and has no other life? At this point even teens recommend that parents step in. As fifteen-year-old Jordan says, "Parents should use time off-screen as a penalty if teenagers don't do their work, especially during exam time." Ginny warns parents to make these assessments before they buy their teen a smartphone. "Parents don't ground kids anymore—they turn off their Internet. But with a smartphone the Internet is always on. If you know your kid is having problems and is hard to control, why would you give them a smartphone? I've seen this among my friends and I don't get it!"

And, if your rules and restrictions are not well negotiated with your teens, they will find workarounds. Ginny tells the story of her seventeen-year-old friend who is addicted to a TV show that she watches obsessively online. "My friend's dad blocked all her sites that relate to the show so she can't access them from her computer. But all that happens is she comes into school early and goes to the computer lab and accesses them there. It's true she is wasting too much time on this show, but his approach isn't working. Her dad should have tried negotiating a solution rather than just blocking the sites." Ginny isn't sure what that solution would look like, but says the starting point would need to be her friend's goals and motivations, not her father's.

However, if Ginny's example seems to be a clear-cut case of a teen wasting time with technology, Pierce Vallieres reminds us of the fine line separating wasting time from practising for life. When Pierce was fourteen years old, he created a *Rubik's Cube* app for Apple that is generating worldwide sales. Now, a year later, he is working on another app based on a popular video game. But if our teen tells us to stop obsessing about her screen time because she's inventing a new application, we need to point out the other part of Pierce's story. Even given those long hours spent online, he still finds time to play baseball, hockey and guitar, and is learning to fly an airplane.[4]

Educating vs. Monitoring

We've been focusing on the number of hours our teens are spending online, but an equally important issue is what they are doing while in cyberspace. Many of them are visiting gambling sites, porn sites or adult chat rooms. They may also be exploring sites that promote illegal activities (drug use, bomb building), or contain violence or hate literature. Parry Aftab, executive director of the non-profit organization WiredSafety (see p. 261 for the URL), writes that while online pornography and sexual content receive much of the focus of parental concern, she is more worried about these other kinds of sites with their anti-social and potentially lethal messages.

According to research done by the Media Awareness Network (see p. 261 for the URL), teenagers think young people should be protected from such sites, and they think parents need to get involved. But they don't think parents should be focusing their energy on controls. Instead, they should be teaching youth how to use the Internet safely and intelligently.⁵ Aftab agrees. Her organization works to keep kids and teens safe in cyberspace by providing them with expertise in safe, secure and responsible interactive technology use. She says, "Parents need to understand that the greatest risk our children face online is being denied access. The Internet is essential to our children's education, future careers and lives." The WiredSafety website has a Q&A section for parents with answers to questions such as "How can I tell if my child is communicating with an Internet predator?" and "What if I find out my child is a cyberbully?" This organization is linked to Wired Kids, Inc. (see p. 261 for the URL) and its website includes a safety guide for parents as well as articles, activities and online safety advice designed by teens for teens.

The Media Awareness Network has a section where parents post their tips for safe Internet use, which include signing an Internet-use contract with their child, keeping the computer in a place of public access, and talking to their children about what they are doing online. Their online game for nine- to twelve-year-olds, called "Cybersense and Nonsense," explores the world of chat rooms, and teaches the player to distinguish between fact and fiction and detect bias and harmful stereotyping in online content.

Parental involvement can make a difference in online behaviour, at least for younger teens. For example, if a household has rules about "sites you should not visit," research shows that young teens are three times less likely than those in households with no rules to deliberately visit sites dealing in porn, gore, hate and related topics.[6] So setting guidelines for teenagers' online activity is important, though it is probably not the rules per se that are critical, but the message those rules send about parental interest and involvement.

The teenagers I interviewed suggest that parents establish the following rules:

- *Be careful about giving personal information online.*
- *Don't submit any type of inappropriate pictures/videos online (e.g., nudity, smoking, breaking any laws/rules).*
- *Don't talk with strangers online, in chat rooms, etcetera.*
- *Don't download files without a parent's knowledge (to avoid viruses).*
- *Realize that what you put online is forever, so be careful with what images you show or what you say about yourself and others.*

But once we've established our rules, how do we make sure they're being followed? Teresa has made the decision to monitor her thirteen-year-old daughter by using a product called eBlaster available through its website (see p. 261 for the URL). "Parents get a daily e-mail report with time online, each website visited and duration of visit, as well as copies of e-mails and IMS [an instant messaging service]," she explains. "While it can seem like 'big brother,' we use it to discuss appropriate and inappropriate Internet activity." Net Nanny is another monitoring product that sits on the user's hard drive and can block undesirable websites. Newer services charge a subscription fee to scan the Web for evidence of what your child is doing online.

I asked Ginny, the seventeen-year-old, for her advice on how to walk the fine line between monitoring and education. She feels that younger people need to be protected from inappropriate images but points out how difficult this is to do, except by parental presence. "I was just googling a topic myself and up popped some disgusting images. I found it really disturbing, even at my age." She tries to be present when her younger niece and nephew, who live across the street, are watching videos on YouTube. "They can accidentally land on something that is really awful. Some of the music videos are really offensive." Her recommendation is that parents spend time with younger teens exploring the Internet together. "More importantly," she says, "parents need to spend time talking with their teens about those tough subjects like sex and drugs. If they aren't talking with their teens and trying to guide them through things, they're going to be searching for the information themselves." Aftab would agree with Ginny. She warns that using monitoring software or services is "no substitute for good parenting techniques, like frequent conversations about Internet activities."[7]

As we decide for ourselves where we stand on the fine line between monitoring and education, we need to remind ourselves that trust is the foundation on which our relationship with our teenagers is built. When we trust them, we invest emotionally in them, and this trust becomes a powerful motivating force. In *Hold On to Your Kids*, Gordon Neufeld and Gabor Maté explain that it is the act of trusting, not the outcome, that must be our focus. They remind us that even if our child is unable to measure up to our expectations or realize his own intentions, we must still trust that he is trying. "To withdraw that trust is to take the wind out of his sails and to hurt him deeply. If the desire to be good for us is not treasured and nurtured, the child will lose his motivation to keep trying to measure up."[8]

The importance of trust was forcefully brought home to me when my daughter gave me a letter on Mother's Day, shortly after she had turned eighteen. The letter was titled "Thank You" and here's what she had to say about trust: "I want to thank you for your ability to treat me as an adult, put your trust in me and in those I trust. For your ability to let me make my own decisions and my own mistakes." Looking back on my own teen years, I think the only time I was seriously untrustworthy was when I attended a school run by a principal who did not trust his students. Since he treated us as though we were going to act irresponsibly at the first opportunity, many of us did. I was eighteen years old and this lack of trust was new for me. Since I was the eldest of three, my parents had relied on me at home, and I had been in the workforce from the age of twelve, as babysitter, camp counsellor and staff at a women's clothing store. I learned a powerful lesson from this man's contempt: teenagers often live down to the expectations of those in authority.

But there are times when you need to *trust but verify*. "By reading my daughter's e-mail I found out she was being harassed by her girlfriends," Eleanor says. "You need to be hyper-vigilant to your teen's moods and behaviour, and when Emma was in grade 9, she seemed depressed, moody and focused on being on MSN[9] constantly. One day I went to her computer and looked at a few things. She had been sloppy, and had saved some messages where it was easy for me to see them. Was it sloppy or a call for help? Turns out the girls had 'ditched' her and were spreading nasty sexual rumours about her. She couldn't stop herself from reading their horrible lies, and she was slipping out of reality. So I banned her from MSN and encouraged her not to cheat on herself by sneaking onto other people's computers. Off and on for the next year, whenever she wanted her MSN privileges back, I became the 'mean mother.' When she was seventeen, she said that banning her from MSN had been the best thing I could have done, and that finding other things to fill the 'hole' was the key to her success. I still think she spends too much time on the computer, but now she doesn't get depressed about it, and I think she has a very healthy self-respect. Trust your teen, but if you need to get at the root of a problem, don't hesitate to do the necessary sleuthing."

If we fear for the safety and well-being of our children, like Eleanor, we need to violate their privacy. It may go against our deeply held principles, but there are times when it's necessary. Another friend of mine found herself in that position when her daughter was caught shoplifting. She decided to read her diary, and the memory is still raw. "I knew it was a violation of some sort of sacred trust between us," she says, "and even now, years later, I feel absolutely awful about it. I've never told her. But I know it was the right thing to do because it helped me understand her state of mind and I was able to help her." So while our emphasis should be on education and trust, if circumstances warrant, we need to hold our nose, cross that line and begin monitoring and verifying.

Fun vs. Obsession

Many parents despair about the amount of time their teenagers spend playing video games, participating in virtual gaming or simply entertaining themselves online. They are in good company. A Pew Research Center poll found that 50 percent of teens in the survey had played video games the previous day.[10] Many of them probably feel they can't help themselves. According to another poll, 23 percent of gamers felt addicted to video games.[11] The problem is particularly acute for boys. They are playing video games an average of eighteen hours a week, as compared to eight hours for girls.[12]

When I asked teenagers what advice parents should give their teens, one of the tips was to restrict the time they spend gaming. Eric says, "Tell your kids not to play the endless role-playing games like *World of Warcraft* because they are a HUGE waste of time." Jordan agrees, "Limit their play of massively time-consuming games or find them a simple game that is fun but doesn't require hours of play."

It's not surprising that Eric singled out *World of Warcraft* (*WoW*). *WoW* holds the Guinness World Record for most subscribers to a MMORPG (massively multi-player online role-playing game), more than twelve million as of December 2010. In *WoW*, players control an avatar (their digital character) and engage in combat with other players, defeat monsters and complete quests. The game setting is a 3D fantasy universe with many similarities to the real world. The play continues whether or not you are present, you can acquire skills that give you higher status along with the potential for amassing resources, and there are banks in which to deposit your treasures. The more demanding tasks or quests require you to collaborate with other players. If your teen gamer is late for dinner, he may not be deliberately flouting your wishes, he may be in the middle of an elaborate raid with fellow players who are depending on his participation.[13]

Addiction to the game is so pervasive that Internet support groups have been set up for *World of Warcraft* "widows." "I have been widowed twice by *WoW*," says my daughter's friend. "Two of my ex-boyfriends were unable to stay away from the game long enough to spend time with me. Both times the relationship broke up because I was unwilling to be stood up because of a computer game. The only thing worse was watching my boyfriend cry because his avatar died. I just didn't get it!" The website wikiHow has a manual on "How to Break a *World of Warcraft* Addiction." Tips include: quit along with your friends since you're just playing to spend time with them, find other diversions such as martial arts, reading or less time-consuming games, and delete your character and sell your account.[14]

In addition to being a widow-maker and time-waster, research has found that excessive online gaming has some unhealthy consequences. A recent study in China found that adolescents who spent excessive amounts of time online reacted very intensely to their successes and failures in the online gaming world and often went long periods without sleep. The study found that otherwise healthy teens were much more vulnerable to depression if they spent too much time on the Internet.[15]

These concerns are real and demand careful monitoring, but there is an upside, too. In *Everything Bad Is Good for You*, Steven Johnson acknowledges the problems with video games but develops a persuasive argument that, by playing them, your teen is becoming a better thinker. Johnson points out that complex video games require real cognitive labour. They force the player to make decisions that require the use of systems analysis, probability theory, pattern recognition and patience. You learn how to use the scientific method of testing hypotheses, and figure out how to develop strategies that keep both short-term and long-term goals in mind. Through the time and effort it takes to get a reward, you also learn about delayed gratification. Most importantly as far as teens are concerned, all this learning happens without you realizing you're being educated.

Constance Steinkuehler, a researcher at the University of Wisconsin-Madison, says virtual games improve a teenager's social skills because they require him to learn how to collaborate, lead a group or self-organize. For example, coordinating a large team of some twenty-five people to carry out a complex raid in a game like *World of Warcraft* could take two to four hours and requires considerable negotiation. She says that virtual games offer players practice in "collective problem-solving, collective information-sharing, and understanding how to find an answer in your social network." She argues that these skills are components of twenty-first-century literacy.[16]

Johnson's and Steinkuehler's arguments focus on the skills acquired from playing a complex video game, rather than what the players learn from the content. But it is a mistake to ignore the game's theme and message. Iowa State University psychologists argue that exposure to violent video games desensitizes people to real-life violence. Their study, which measured physiological responses such as heartbeat rates and galvanic skin responses, found that college students' reactions to scenes of real violence differed significantly as a result of having just played a violent or a non-violent game. They concluded that individuals who play violent video games get used to the violence and become physiologically numb to it.[17]

If you are worried that your teen is consuming an excessive amount of violent media—movies, music, television and video games—and is displaying aggressive or depressive behaviour, there is an online *Checklist for Violent Youth* developed by the National School Safety Center (NSSC) in the United States to identify signs of potential violence.

These warning signals could indicate a youth's potential for harming him/herself or others, and parents are urged to make sure their teen's mental health needs are being addressed through school, medical or social service counselling.[18]

The website ParentFurther (see p. 261 for the URL) has a number of resources to help you understand more about the games your teen wants to play and whether you should be worried. More and more of the most popular games are rated "M for mature" (intended for adults seventeen years or older). The website includes a guide that explains the meanings of these video game ratings by the Entertainment Software Ratings Board (ESRB). Their guide to video game terminology includes definitions such as *griefer*: a person who torments new players by bullying or harassing them. Their *Guide to Video Game Addiction* lists symptoms to watch out for, as well as self-assessment surveys, one for the parent to complete and one for the child. The guide includes the following quote from a high-school student. "Computer games are ruining my life. If I'm not playing, I'm thinking about playing. I have, like, no real friends."[19]

Jane dealt with her sixteen-year-old son's attraction to the virtual gaming world by strictly limiting his access to his Xbox. "David loves to play games with his virtual friends all over the world, and, if I let him, he'd be at it day and night. I could see that he was completely incapable of controlling how much time he spent on the Xbox, so I told him he could only play with it on weekends. But he kept using it anyway, so I locked it away in the house. Even then he would find the key. By this point I realized that 'just weekend use' was still too much, so now he's only allowed to use it on vacations. It's completely hidden away in a place where he can't find it, and only emerges during holidays. The most interesting thing about this battle is how willing he was to accept the current regime. There were no tantrums. It seems he's relieved that the temptation has been removed—because he couldn't control it himself!

"There are several aspects of the virtual gaming world that worry me," Jane says. "The obvious problem is simple: if you're spending all that time playing online games there are a whole bunch of things you don't have time for—school work, sports, spending time with 'real' friends, not to mention your family. But then there's the fact that I don't know these virtual friends. What are they like? Would I want David to hang out with them if I knew them face to face? And what values are these games teaching? Are they values that I would support? And then there's the whole thing about 'the latest and the greatest.' You're getting sucked into a money pit paying gaming fees and wanting upgrades with the newest version of games. It never ends. So at the very least, my son is now spending less time, and hopefully less money, on an activity that I'm uncomfortable with."

A friend who is now in his twenties spent a good number of hours immersed in a virtual gaming world when he was in his teens, and I asked him what he thought about Jane's concerns. Steve figures that, between the ages of ten and fifteen, he spent about two to three hours a day in online role-playing games. Here's what he has to say. "Looking back, I don't think the experience did me any harm. I would tell Jane not to worry too much about the other virtual players—at least in the games I played—because the content of the game is so constraining you never really get to know one another. Remember, the gaming world is very different from a social-networking site—at least it was then. But I would have to agree that spending so much time on any one activity, this one included, does lead to missed opportunities. And I think those could be quite considerable; and I certainly feel they were in my case. It's difficult to speculate what else I might have done with all that time—maybe write a play, get more involved in politics, fall in love. So given that there is a tremendous societal pull for teenagers towards electronic existence, I think a parental push towards other kinds of pursuits is a useful counterweight."

It's important to remember that there are a variety of video games and a range of ways to play them. Some approaches to gaming actually bring people together—in the flesh. Marilyn's teens play video games in a group. "They share tips or 'cheats' and discuss strategies for succeeding at the game," she says. "Although I worry about the amount of time they spend online, overall, gaming has been a social and co-operative activity for them, with the competition residing in the game." Some families play video games as a togetherness activity. In the case of our family, at large extended-family events that include people of all ages, we've had great fun gathered around the TV screen playing virtual tennis and bowling.

The fine line between fun and addiction is a familiar one for adults because we're struggling to walk it ourselves. My friend Liz just removed *Solitaire* and *Sudoku* from her iPhone. "My behaviour was addictive," she confessed. "When I found myself playing games in the washroom at work, then I knew I was in trouble. So I removed them from my phone."

But while we need to teach our teens ways of controlling their online obsessions, we have to acknowledge that it's human to entertain ourselves, and the Internet gives us a whole new world of opportunities. I enjoy wasting time reading online jokes and watching hilarious YouTube videos. And then there's the ROFL universe. ROFL stands for "rolling on the floor, laughing," and there is no other purpose for participants than to create things on the Internet that are funny and weird, like absurdly captioned pictures of cats. They do it just because it's fun.[20]

Multi-tasking vs. Inability to Focus

Because technology allows our teens to multi-task constantly, we worry they have lost the capacity to focus and are no longer capable of being fully in the moment. You're in the middle of an important discussion with your daughter and all of a sudden her phone vibrates or her computer pings and her attention instantly shifts away from you to her digital device. She says, "I'm still listening, Dad. I can do more than one thing at a time you know." But can she? Many studies have shown that disruption interferes with learning, and we're not as good as we think at doing two things at once. We just have to look at the ban on driving and cellphone use in many jurisdictions for evidence that people can't drive safely and talk on a cellphone at the same time. And just try to pat your head while you're rubbing your stomach and see how much concentration is required.

In his book *The Shallows*, Nicholas Carr argues that the more we multi-task, the more our skills for sustained concentration and deep thinking erode. He sees the problem as more than a temporary glitch: he argues that our brains are being rewired in response to the wired world. "Calm, focused, undistracted, the linear mind is being pushed aside by a new kind of mind that wants and needs to take in and dole out information in short, disjointed, often overlapping bursts—the faster, the better."[21] In order to maintain the kind of concentration Carr felt he needed to write *The Shallows*, he moved to the mountains and disconnected himself from the wired world.

While there is clearly a downside to having a scattered mind, the ability to multi-task will be a skill required in the workplaces of the future, and many require it now. When Apple's senior vice-president was let go from his job in the summer of 2010 it was reported that he wasn't able "to think outside the box." He had come from IBM and wasn't used to Apple's corporate culture where "even senior executives are expected to keep on top of the smallest details of their area of responsibility and often have to handle many tasks directly, as opposed to delegating them."[22]

Ideally, our teens should be able to access, as required, both minds that Carr describes—the linear mind and the "new kind of mind." Since the bias of the online world is towards the new mind, our teens are likely acquiring those skills as a matter of course. Our work lies in teaching them how to be able to tap into Carr's "calm, focused, undistracted" mind whenever they need to utilize its strengths.

Poor school performance is often the warning signal that our teenager is having trouble focusing. In her book, *That Crumpled Paper Was Due Last Week*, academic counsellor Ana Homayoun tells the story of Adam, a fifteen-year-old who was floundering at school and spending four hours a night on Facebook. She convinced him to do his homework first, before succumbing to other distractions on the computer. After he had finished his homework, he could go on Facebook, but had to use a kitchen timer to track his time. "At first, give yourself a whole hour," she said. "Go to all the sites you want, leave messages on people's walls, send e-mails, whatever. Concentrate your time on the computer so that what you once spent four hours doing you can now get done in an hour."[23] Adam is now down to thirty minutes a day. Homayoun's book provides tips on how to help your teen get organized, learn how to study, and most importantly, learn how to set personal goals. Her book stresses the importance of routine: finding a consistent place to study (ideally away from the bedroom), creating a scheduled block of time for homework that is free from technological distractions, and building in active time before sitting down to work.

Barbara has used these same strategies with her son. "I've suggested he work on homework, without giving in to distractions, for a manageable amount of time, say an hour, then reward himself with a break, say twenty minutes," she says. "That way he can finish his homework earlier, turn the computer off, or better yet remove it from his room and curl up with a book like he used to. I believe his computer use is affecting his sleep. He goes to bed much later than he used to, but claims he simply can't fall asleep early anymore. This change in sleep habits may have everything to do with being a teenager, but it also seems to coincide with having his own computer, and being allowed to use it in his room. He readily admits that while he is doing homework, he is easily distracted by all the other options on his computer. This means he uses it later into the night in order to complete his homework, and is exposed to the bright light for a longer period of time. We've talked about the studies suggesting that light emitted from laptops, smartphones and iPads can be bright enough to disturb your circadian rhythm [the clock in your brain that determines when you sleep and when you wake up]. All these discussions are a work in progress."

Research supports Barbara's concern that her son's ability to focus would improve with more sleep. Homayoun found that students who were able to implement her time-management advice were able to complete their schoolwork faster and go to bed earlier. After getting more hours of sleep, her students were calmer, more focused and less stressed. As for Barbara's concerns about the bright lights of the computers disturbing her son's circadian rhythm, the jury is still out. While individuals report this finding from their own experience, no research has been done specifically on whether laptops disrupt sleep cycles.[24] But it stands to reason that bright lights and stimulation make it harder to fall asleep, so our teen's digital devices should be turned off at a reasonable hour and kept off. The teens I interviewed are well aware of this link between sleep deprivation and technology. Their tips for parents: *Tell your teen that if you spend too much time online you're not going to get enough sleep. And turn off your phone at night unless you want to get a text message at 3 A.M. and have your sleep interrupted.*

To help your teen learn to focus, Eleanor recommends *The 7 Habits of Highly Effective Teens.* Sean Covey wrote the book to help teens get their act together and modelled it after the best-selling *The 7 Habits of Highly Effective People* written by his father, Stephen Covey. "My husband gave the book to our son at just the right time," Eleanor says. "He devoured it and followed the instructions to the letter: planning, focusing, living who you are, do not compromise." The seven habits Covey advocates are be proactive; begin with the end in mind; put first things first; think win-win; seek first to understand, then to be understood; synergize; and sharpen the saw (i.e., have your tools in good shape). The book uses stories of real teens and has step-by-step guides. There is a companion workbook. But the book doesn't work for everyone. My daughter received Covey's book from an adult friend and claims proudly to have never read it. Instead she bought herself *The Habits of Seven Highly Annoying People* by Bad Dog Press. It's a hilarious spoof, and reading this book out loud with your teen is a great way to come at the issues from another angle.

To my mind, the best way to counterbalance the seduction of technological multi-tasking is to periodically force our teens to drop out, turn off and engage in activities that require single-minded focus. One effective way to unplug our teens is to get them involved in sports. In her book *Child's Play: Rediscovering the Joy of Play in Our Families and Communities*, Olympic medallist Silken Laumann argues that sports, and play in general, can teach our children how to be fully engaged. "They are figuring out how to keep themselves busy when they feel bored; they are learning that effort translates into increased competence, and that increased competence leads to increased enjoyment. I want my kids to have dreams, and to possess the discipline needed to fulfill those dreams."[25] As an added bonus, teenagers who play sports are far less likely to smoke or use drugs. "This is not just because they are busy," Laumann writes, "but because when we use our bodies to run and jump and play, we have a deeper respect for our physical selves."[26]

The Youth Olympic Games has a program to encourage young people to get away from the computer screen and into athletic endeavours. One of their strategies is "The Best of Us Challenge," a contest that lets youth compete with some of the world's top athletes by video-recording their own performance. For example, Carolina Klüft, the

Swedish track and field champ, challenges youth to the Handstick Distance Walk to see in thirty seconds how many steps they can take walking on their hands. Young people upload videos that record their responses to these challenges or create their own challenges.[27]

Summer camps are another great way for teenagers to disconnect, as long as you find one that restricts cellphone and computer use. "Summer camp was transformative for my son," Marilyn says. "He gained confidence and maturity, was recognized with awards and given responsibility, and got seriously interested in guitar. I suspect there was some romance, too." Both my daughters went to camp in their early teens and they can list the skills they acquired, as well as the trials and tribulations from the swarming mosquitoes, gruelling swimming tests and exhausting canoe trips. I vividly remember my own camp adventures, especially the summer I was sixteen, which included a fourteen-day canoe trip where we were lost (for no more than a day), a bear incident involving our food pack, and the boat-swamping conditions I overcame to pass my master canoeist exam—all impossible to replicate online. But camp experiences are fully engaging only if there is minimal connection to the online world.

Three-quarters of the camps that are accredited by the American Camp Association (ACA) ban e-mail, cellphones and computers. As the past president of ACA says, "Camp is an opportunity to unplug and develop authentic relationships." These unplugged camps encourage letter writing, and it has to be done the old-fashioned way. One camper, who typically writes during rest hour in her cabin, says she finds the process "sort of peaceful."[28] If you're looking for a camp for your teenager, the websites www.mysummer-camps.com and www.camps.ca have information on thousands of camps in North America and around the world, including academic, arts, sports and special-needs camps.

For Hannah, it was sailing that provided her two sons with fully engaging experiences. "Sailing has the advantage of being a sport where you have to be completely focused because there is real risk. The whole point is to go as fast as you can, and there are no brakes. You have to be able to steer through all kinds of tough conditions, and there's a real danger of injuring yourself. You can damage your boat or you can fall out, and these things did happen to them. On a really windy day the boys would come back from sailing and there would be lots of adrenalin. They became more and more capable of coping with situations that would have frightened them before. And they knew it."

Getting your teen involved in the arts, whether music, dance, fine art, writing or theatre, can be an antidote to multi-tasking and distraction. Artistic endeavours require practice, which needs focus, and all those rehearsals are hours spent away from the computer. When Eleanor looked back on her own teen years, she realized that her parents used music lessons to prepare her for adult life, because there were consequences. "My mother and father gave me responsibilities to live up to," she says, "including musical recitals that would have flopped if I had not practised. My music lessons helped me develop a respect for competition, and taught me that winning was not the only desired outcome. They died in a car accident when I was twenty, and looking back they prepared me perfectly for life."

When it comes to the fine line between multi-tasking and ability to focus, on balance I'm in Steven Johnson's camp. He's the author of *Everything Bad Is Good for You*, whose work I referred to earlier. He agrees that, like any new experience, the use of technology to multi-task is changing our brains. He argues, however, that the benefits are worth it. On the plus side, the Internet has increased by several orders of magnitude the speed with which we can follow the trail of an idea or discover new perspectives on a problem. The way he sees it, society makes its advances not just from solitary effort, but from the connective space, "in the collision of different worldviews and sensibilities, different metaphors and fields of expertise." His conclusion: "We are marginally less focused, and exponentially more connected. That's a bargain all of us should be happy to make."[29]

But like with so many of these fine lines, the truth lies in the balance. We still need to be able to tap into that "calm, focused, undistracted" mind that Nicholas Carr talks about, and our children need to be taught how. Recently, a technological college in Pennsylvania took the bold step of blacking out social media for a week. While on campus, neither students nor staff could access social-network sites including Facebook and Twitter. The exercise was done to get people to think critically about the prevalence of social media, and the exercise seems to have been successful. During the blackout, one student, who found she was freed from toggling between her social-networking sites and her course work, said, "Now I can just solely focus." But it was her assessment of the experiment that really impressed me. Instead of interpreting the blocking of technology as a reactionary move, she saw it as a demonstration of the university's focus on innovation.[30]

I hope this attitude is a precursor of the future. I would like to see programs for stilling the multi-tasking mind made a standard part of the school curriculum. For many years now, I have used yoga and meditation to help calm my racing brain and allow me to tap into a deeper level of concentration. One day when my daughter was particularly frantic, I taught her the simple yoga exercise of alternate-nostril breathing. Although she doesn't practise it, we use it as an ongoing joke whenever things are getting out of hand for either of us, as in "Why don't you go do some alternate-nostril breathing!" She is now attuned to the use of meditation as an alternative to prescription drugs, and has counselled friends who were looking for stress relief. While we're waiting for our schools to implement yoga and meditation courses, you'll find many websites with step-by-step instructions, including www.hathayogalesson.com.

Staying the Course vs. Dropping Out

In the past most of us attended the neighbourhood high school, but today's teenagers, especially those in urban centres, have a choice among secondary schools that emphasize different strengths, whether sports, creative arts, academics or religious instruction, and the digital world is making it easier to send our children farther afield. Because our teens are able to stay in online contact with their school friends, we are less worried that distance will cut them off socially, or that we'll become the chauffeur on-call. And when even teens in the same neighbourhood find it easier to meet on Skype to work together on school projects, we don't feel as though we're disadvantaging our children by living far from their classmates.

I've been involved in countless hours of discussion with parents as we try to figure out what would be the best school for our teenager. We worry about these decisions because they matter—both for our child's immediate happiness, and for their future success. Research has found that our best bet is to find a school with the following qualities: well resourced, provides education that is accepting, sets limits and has high expectations for students.[31] Another criteria should be the extent to which the school uses digital tools to support good pedagogy. Woodside High School would make a good benchmark. This public school in Silicon Valley obtained $3 million in grants for a multimedia centre and the principal is luring students off their cellphones and video games by fighting fire with fire. Music recording is taught using digital tools, iPads are employed to teach Mandarin and teachers use websites to communicate with students. But the principal is implementing his digital strategy with full awareness that the "unchecked use of digital devices can create a culture in which students are addicted to the virtual world and lost in it."[32]

If you'd like some assistance evaluating schools, the website www.ourkids.net/school/ contains a directory of private schools in the United States and Canada including alternative schools, faith-based schools and schools for special-needs or gifted children. There are articles on choosing the right school for your family, and suggestions on questions to ask the schools. Most of the resources are equally applicable for choosing among publicly funded schools.

When you're searching for schools I would add another criterion that will be harder to assess: the school should be "a good fit" for your child and your family. It was Naomi, a wise young woman, who alerted me to the importance of this factor. As a teenager, her school and her home life had been at polar ends of the conservative–liberal values spectrum. She had experienced a great deal of anxiety trying to reconcile the elitist values of her high school with the left-leaning views of her family. She finally changed schools to find a learning atmosphere that was more compatible with her home life. She advised my husband and me to pay attention to the school culture when picking schools for our daughters.

Although I thought we had acted on this advice, our daughter also ended up changing schools midway through high school in order to find a place where she felt more at home. After three years at her first school, she was doing well academically but felt restricted by the teaching style and atmosphere. Her unhappiness was palpable so we supported her decision to switch into a specialized arts program at another school. Here she found a learning environment that was more compatible with her worldview. The result was a happier, more engaged young woman who graduated with top marks. Our decision to go along with her desire to change schools was questioned by some of our friends. Two of them had daughters of the same age who were equally unhappy at their schools, but, in both cases, they insisted that their daughters stick it out. They felt that, at fifteen years of age, they lacked the judgement to appreciate the full implications of such a move.

We decided to use the opportunity to model decision-making, and worked with our daughter to set objectives, identify the schools that met our criteria, tour the schools on our short list and analyze their pros and cons. When she was successful at being accepted into the school of her choice, through a tough audition process, she recognized that it was a significant achievement. It demonstrated to her the confidence the school had in her potential and the extent of her personal strength. She looks back now, happy with her decision, and is able to acknowledge what she gained from her experiences—at both schools. Sadly, both of my friends' daughters did end up leaving their schools—but because of illness rather than choice. One developed bulimia, and the other had a mental-health crisis. Both young women have since worked through their problems, and my friends have no way of knowing whether switching schools would have changed the outcomes, but they wonder.

Gloria also found that choosing the right school for your child is not an easy matter. She learned the hard way that your son or daughter must be onside with the decision, or it's not going to work out. "I basically forced my son to attend a private school when he was in grade 5, and it completely backfired. I had to withdraw him after two months because he was depressed, and both his pediatrician and a social worker from whom I sought counselling told me I had made a big mistake. This experience was transformative for me. I learned that forcing my son into things does not work. And, now, instead of focusing on all the things I wish he were doing, I really try to focus on all the things he is doing right."

Once our teens are in school, the challenge is to keep them there, particularly if they're boys.[33] The main reasons that boys give for quitting are school-related: being bored, problems with schoolwork and with teachers and being "kicked out." And some of them leave because they want or need to work.[34] Experts offer a variety of explanations for why boys are falling behind in school, including developmental differences, a lack of role models, feminization of education and the "boy code" that treats asking for help as weakness. They also speculate that video games have a role to play. One study found that boys aged six to nine who had a video-gaming system at home spent less time doing homework, reading for fun or being read to by parents, and their reading and writing scores were significantly lower than those without the games.[35]

Jordan, who is eighteen years old and in his first year of university, found when he was younger that his video-game obsession had a big impact on his schoolwork. Gaming for two to four hours per day in high school took precedence over homework for this former "A" student. The games were a great escape from courses like calculus, and it was thrilling to compete against players from all over the world. When he found he was failing chemistry, the combination of his parents "nagging" and an inspiring biology class turned him around. But it was his parents' grim predictions that really made him buckle down. As he told the *Globe and Mail*, "They painted pictures of a future without an education, and it was some place I didn't want to be." He found he didn't need to quit playing video games to boost his marks. "I just smartened up with my time management," he said.[36]

When Bev's son was doing badly in high school, she and her husband worked with the school to set up a support system to get him back on track. "When my son, John, was fifteen years old," she says, "I got a call from his school saying they wanted to schedule a meeting to discuss his dismal performance. John had been skipping classes, failing to hand in assignments and doing badly on tests. Looking back, he was probably struggling with some learning issues, but, then, all we knew was that he was completely unmotivated. What happened at the meeting changed John's life, and I give full credit to his teacher. The outcome of the meeting was a three-way agreement negotiated among John, us [his parents] and the school. John's dream was to visit his sister in Barbados during summer holidays, and this was the carrot that we used to change his behaviour. John's teacher proposed a system of credits for desired actions (e.g., turning assignments in on time, passing grades, etcetera). He would communicate John's performance to us, and we would turn the credits into dollars towards the trip. If John changed his mind about visiting his sister, the dollars could be used for another trip, but not turned into cash. John's performance was transformed, and I think it was all due to the structure and clarity of this agreement, coupled with the support of the teacher—not to mention the lure of the prized trip."

Bev's story and the successful strategy her family implemented could have come straight from the book *The Minds of Boys: Saving Our Sons From Falling Behind in School and Life* by Michael Gurian and Kathy Stevens, which is a useful resource if your son has a learning disability or is underperforming at school. The chapter on what parents and teachers can do to motivate boys to learn is full of specific techniques, including using tutors, masters and apprentices, providing attention from the extended family, generating positive attention among parent-led teams and professionals, regulating what your son watches and eats, doing homework together and using rites of passage such as the driver's licence to motivate.

If you are worried that, like John, your teenager may have a learning disability, there are a number of online resources to assist you, including the website of the Learning Disabilities Association of America (see p. 262 for the URL). The Learning Disabilities Association of Ontario (URL also on p. 262) has a website with frequently asked questions from young people and their parents about learning disabilities.

When I asked teenagers to tell me their big issues around school, I was struck by the number of times they complained about being forced to identify job aspirations and chart career paths long before they were ready. They feel intense pressure to know where they're going and how they're going to get there—and they don't have the answers. My niece, Natalie, says she was grateful for my advice when, at the age of seventeen, her academic advisors told her she had to start specializing, so she needed to choose between arts and science. She was torn by this decision, and I well understood her dilemma. She is a gifted artist who also excelled at her science courses, and she seemed to get equal enjoyment from both. She asked me to help her make the choice. It seemed completely unreasonable to me that she should have to narrow her options at such a young age, so I encouraged her to continue to take courses in both arts and science in high school, and then find a university that would allow her to do the same.

Looking back, she says it was what I said next that helped her the most. She reminded me that when I proposed this dual stream approach she worried out loud, "But when they ask me what I'm going to do with these courses, and what I'm going to become, what am I going to say?" I replied, "Tell them your job hasn't been invented yet. In the mid-sixties, if I had told my guidance counsellor that my business card was going to read 'consultant in the applications of learning technologies,' neither of us would have had a clue what that meant." Natalie did pursue both arts and science, and was one of a handful of students accepted into a highly coveted graduate program that gave her a degree in biomedical communications—a program she didn't even know existed until she was twenty-one. Currently she is working with a team of medical professionals as a medical illustrator and digital media designer, a job that uses both her artistic and her scientific talents and passions.

As our teens figure out their best options for careers in the digital world, we need to work with their schools to support them. Traditional occupations are changing, brand new fields are opening up and some jobs have become economically viable thanks to the Internet, which allows the exponential expansion of some markets. There are countless examples of the Internet turning formerly marginal pastimes into careers, but one of my favourites was provided by a woman I met at a historical site, where she was playing the role of a landlady in a boarding house circa 1890. She was an expert on the food, drink and social mores of the late 1800s, as well as a very good actor. After her performance we had a chance to talk, and I was amazed when she told me she was able to find enough historical re-enactment gigs that required a specialist in her era to generate a full-time income. What made this possible for her was a website that connects suppliers and purchasers in the re-enactment community. And she added, in the interests of full disclosure, that she had a supplementary source of income—making clothing and accessories for other actors who were portraying this era. Another equally marginal occupation, I would not have imagined prior to our discussion.

The Social Teen

Sharing vs. Indiscretion

WHEN our teenagers are online they are often walking a fine line between "sharing" and indiscretion, and may not understand that even seemingly harmless activities can have consequences. Teenagers need to be taught that privacy on the Internet should never be assumed, and that the online world has a long memory. The teenagers I interviewed recommend that parents make the rules as clear-cut as possible: *Don't submit any type of inappropriate picture/video online (e.g., nudity, smoking, breaking any laws/rules). Realize that what you put online is forever, so be careful with what images you show or what you say about others.*

We need to warn our teens that in the future, when they are applying for a job, a research grant or even a visa to enter a country,[1] their online profile will probably be reviewed. A recent study found that, before making a hiring decision, 79 percent of hiring managers and job recruiters review an applicant's online information, and 70 percent had rejected candidates based on what they found.[2] So what our teens say or do online could come back to haunt them, whether it's a message on a social-networking site, a blog or Twitter, or an image they upload to photo- or video-sharing sites or swap on cellphones.

To bring the issue home, we could tell our teens the story of Stacy Snyder, the twenty-five-year-old teacher-in-training from Pennsylvania who was denied her degree after she posted a photo of herself on her MySpace page with the caption "drunken pirate." In the photo she is wearing a pirate hat and drinking from a large yellow plastic cup. The school officials felt the image was unprofessional and might promote underage drinking.[3]

And then there was Kimberley Swann, the sixteen-year-old British girl who complained about her office job on Facebook, including the words "im so totally bord [*sic*]!!!" When her employer found out what she had written, she was fired. Her response: "I didn't even put the company's name, I just put that my job was boring. They were just being nosy, going through everything. I think it is really sad, it makes them look stupid that they are going to be so petty." Here's how her employer saw it. "We were looking for a long-term relationship with Miss Swann as we do with all our staff. Her display of disrespect and dissatisfaction undermined the relationship and made it untenable."[4] The lesson for our teens is that something they may view as a casual comment or a playful image made in private could become public and be perceived as a sign of their character.

But these examples may be too far removed from our teen's day-to-day existence to assist him when he is confronted with an immediate opportunity to act without thinking. In his book *Teen Brain, Teen Mind*, Dr. Ron Clavier explains that because the teenage brain is not fully developed it lacks the *time* dimension. Only the "here and now" exists for teenagers, and they aren't able to fully envision the future consequences of their actions. Barbara found this out when she tried to remind her fifteen-year-old son that what he posted on Facebook remains in cyberspace forever. "We do periodically remind our son of the permanency of the digital footprint, but it doesn't always sink in," she says. "Luckily, since I'm his 'friend' on Facebook, I was able to see something he had written himself, and talk about the problem right then and there." Here's Barbara's story: "My son went to a birthday party that a good friend of mine was holding for her daughter. He knew few people there, was miserable and made no effort to socialize. He spent the evening playing on his phone and when he came home, promptly went on Facebook and announced what a horrible time he had at this 'boring, lame' event. When I saw what he wrote I was livid because this could potentially have been seen by any number of his seven-hundred-plus 'friends.' But I knew he had acted impulsively, with no thought to the consequences. I reminded him that the girl in question and her brother were both friends of his and could see what he wrote. This had been a very special event for the girl and her family, and he should have had the ability to handle his feelings in a more mature and responsible manner. I explained to him that if this had happened to me as a teenager, the most I could have done was phone a friend and complain, and maybe a few others would have found out through word of mouth. While this is no better than posting on Facebook, the ability for news to spread is on a completely different level. He felt very remorseful, apologized and promptly removed what he had posted. He said he just needed to vent, but didn't think about how easily this girl could have found out, and how hurtful his actions could have been. This had not been his intention."

And what about those suggestive photos our teens are posting online? They aren't X-rated, but they do make us uncomfortable. Convincing teens that flamboyant self-portrayals and images of provocative posturing are inappropriate is a tough message to convey. "My daughter simply doesn't believe this is an issue," says Marilyn. "The pressure—or maybe it's a youthful impulse—to test one's personal attractiveness by attempting 'sexy' looks and poses is frighteningly strong."

If the argument that your teen's digital reputation could live forever isn't persuasive, another approach is to focus on "false advertising." You could point out that the message your teen is giving may not match his intentions. When Helen's young teenage daughter started dressing in a way that was highly provocative, Helen wanted her to understand that she was going to get lots of unwanted attention from the opposite sex. "So one day I came down to the breakfast table dressed similarly. My daughter said, 'You're not going to work like that, are you?' I replied, 'Why not?'

We then had a great discussion about the kind of impression she thought I was going to make on people. She came to the very conclusion I hoped she would—people wouldn't be able to get past what I was wearing to find out what kind of a person I really was. Sometimes a lesson is best taught in the flesh!"

Another approach is to enlist admired older siblings or friends in the cause. When Susan saw her younger sister's provocative photos on Facebook she gently let her know that they presented her in a very bad light. "I tried to approach the subject very delicately but, even so, she bristled at my interference. I'm not sure I was entirely successful, but I did notice that the worst of the photos were gone last time I looked."

But our ever-inventive teens are using a variety of techniques to remove themselves from the disapproving gaze. Their social-networking site can be set to allow only certain friends (and not their parents) to have access to certain sections, and some teens create a second Facebook account under a different name using an alias that only their friends know. As Susan says, "Now my sister will probably just restrict me to certain parts of her site, but hopefully she'll only show the worst images to a very few of her closest friends."

But even if these "private" postings are protected from nosy adults and future employers, the images and words are still making an impression on the teen's peers. We may have some impact on restraining inappropriate sharing by reminding our teens of this fact. What will that new boyfriend think of your passionate embrace with the old boyfriend? Will the vegan girl you want to impress be grossed out by the video of the puking that followed the "all-you-can-eat barbecue" contest? Will your nasty comments turn off potential friends who fear your poison pen might some day be turned on them?

Peers can have a powerful impact on regulating online behaviour, and the following story from the birth of blogging might be a good reminder. In his book *Say Everything*, Scott Rosenberg tells the tale of Justin Hall, a computer geek who at the age of nineteen became one of the first bloggers. This was 1994, and Justin "invented oversharing" by posting daily about the minutiae of his life, including nude photos of himself, and what Rosenberg calls "a vast amount of material that was in at best questionable taste."[5] But one day Justin abruptly stopped exposing himself online. He fell in love and his young woman gave him an ultimatum: he could not write about her on his website. "And what I discovered is it's very hard to maintain relationships and write in public," Justin concluded. "I decided in the end I would rather have relationships."[6]

Sexting vs. Criminal Behaviour

Using a cellphone to send sexually explicit photographs is called "sexting," and more than 20 percent of teens are estimated to have participated in this activity. In many jurisdictions, sexting is considered to be child pornography and our teens could be prosecuted. This warning comes from

Michael Helfand, an Illinois attorney who says we need to warn our children that it is not only illegal to send these photos, it is illegal to request them from someone else. "Most importantly," he writes, "if they receive a sexually explicit photo, they should delete it from their phone right away. Simply having the photo on your phone could get you in trouble. And passing it along to others is not only illegal, but it could lead to civil liability for invasion of privacy or defamation."[7] In some jurisdictions, punishing sexting among teens as child pornography is viewed as too harsh, and laws are being developed to treat certain cases as misdemeanours, but still as illegal activities, nonetheless.

In some situations, sexting deserves the full force of the law, such as the case, mentioned earlier, of the young man who circulated images of a drugged sixteen-year-old girl being gang-raped. He was charged under Canadian law with possession and distribution of child pornography. Other situations, like the one told to me by sixteen-year-old Stephanie, would benefit more from parental, rather than legal intervention. "A girl I know at school did a striptease on a webcam for a boy," Stephanie says. "He took pictures and showed them around. The girl tried to say it didn't happen and that the boy had 'Photoshopped' the picture. No one believed her because she had done this before."

Then there is Marilyn's story. "The parents of my daughter's friend found highly inappropriate messages on their daughter's computer," Marilyn says. "They included not one but two different instances where boys had sent videocams of themselves masturbating and ejaculating—in one case while some unidentified girl took off her clothes. Our daughter knew one of the boys. It gave us a chance to talk with her about the misuse of electronic communications and about privacy. And I let her know how contemptuous and tasteless and idiotic such behaviour was, and that I hoped that she would never accept it or laugh it off, and tell us about it should it ever occur to her."

It's difficult as parents to make sense of this kind of behaviour, but an understanding of what's happening to the teenage brain at puberty can help. As we discussed, teens are not able to fully envision the future consequences of their actions. And the brains of boys and girls react differently to teenage stresses. In *The Female Brain*, neuropsychiatrist Louann Brizendine writes, "Girls begin to react more to relationship stresses and boys to challenges to their authority. Relationship conflict is what drives a teen girl's stress system wild. She needs to be liked and socially connected; a teen boy needs to be respected and higher in the male pecking order."[8] What this means when it comes to sexting is that boys often use this type of sexual behaviour to impress their friends, and that girls who are desperate to be liked can be persuaded to participate.

How do we make sure that our teens don't act out their stresses in this way? If you ask the police, they have a simple solution: webcams should be ruled out completely for young people. Their concern is that pedophiles are trolling the Internet for visual material, and young people lack the judgement to appreciate how their images might be appropriated and misused. And we can see from these examples that teens can misuse the technology as well. However, simply banning the use of webcams is becoming more challenging because they are built into newer computers, and many cellphones have photo and video capacity.

Also, video chats are becoming a popular technique for keeping far-flung families in touch. Even when relatives live nearby, it can be easier to get your teens to make a cyber-visit than to hold out for "face time." Frances Kaplan's teenage grandsons live in the same city, but she stays connected using Skype and iChat. The seventeen-year-old grandson sends her links to his latest films on YouTube and she gives him feedback via webcam, and the fifteen-year-old helps her troubleshoot her computer problems via video chat.[9] And teens are increasingly using these tools for school work. Seventeen-year-old Ashley says that she and her friends do their group projects using iChat and Skype because it's easier than trying to get everyone together in the same room.

But teens are not only using videocams to talk to Grandma, and when they circulate offensive and overtly sexual material, as in Marilyn and Stephanie's examples, there is a clear need for parents to intervene. I asked Stephanie, who told me the striptease story, whether she is allowed to use a webcam. "I use a webcam to Skype with my sisters who live in different cities," she explained, "as well as with my very close friends. My parents trust me to use my judgement. Plus the door to the room where I use the webcam is always open so they come in and out and can watch what I'm doing."

What if it's too late for supervision and warnings, and your teen has truly crossed the line, like Rennie's young friend whose compromising story introduced the book? We don't know how broadly her photo was circulated, whether it was tagged with her name (allowing a search engine to pull it up), or whether her face was sufficiently visible that some facial recognition scanner could locate it. And the same goes for the young man in the photo. Let's hope for both their sakes that the image is deeply buried in cyberspace. As parents we want to use this story as a cautionary tale and emphasize the inappropriate behaviour of everyone involved.

But if this does happen to our teen, we need to reassure them that life is not over. First, they are far from alone. On Facebook, which is but one of the myriad ways of posting personal information online, there are more than 500 million users who are sharing more than 30 billion pieces of content each month.[10] No doubt, lots of this content is questionable—to someone! Many people (and companies) are keen to wipe their reputations clean, and services such as Reputation.com (see p. 262 for the URL) have sprung up with the promise to remove your personal information from the Web and manage your online reputation. The services they offer include a custom search of the Web, including more than forty social-networking sites, looking for every reference to you, and removal of your personal information wherever possible. A customer is quoted on the website, explaining that he or she used Reputation.com "because the personal evolution I made from college to career was not reflected online." The quote was made anonymously, of course.

Jeffrey Rosen writes in the *New York Times* that technology offers promising solutions to the problem of embarrassing-but-true online information, including the use of expiration dates to wipe the data slate clean. He cites the example of TigerText, an application that allows text-message senders to set a time limit from one minute to thirty days, after which the text disappears from the companies' servers on which it is stored, and therefore from the senders' and recipients' phones. Another product in development is Vanish; it makes data self-destruct by shattering the encryption code. Rosen sounds like a parent when he says, "We need to explore ways of preemptively making the offending words or pictures disappear."[11] In his book *Delete: The Virtue of Forgetting in the Digital Age*, Viktor Mayer-Schönberger emphasizes the value of a fresh digital start. In this way "our society accepts that human beings evolve over time, that we have the capacity to learn from past experiences and adjust our behaviour."[12]

I sincerely hope that Rennie's young acquaintance does not believe that she is all washed up at age fourteen because of an impulsive act that was exacerbated by uncaring friends. We are living on a much more public stage, where many people are watching, and most of us have a performance or two to regret. As fifteen-year-old Sean says, "You live and learn in life. All of you parents have had ample time to learn from your mistakes. In this day and age most mistakes occur online." And if we were to become an online victim, we would have something to learn from the gang-raped sixteen-year-old girl whose images were circulated. She returned to school about a week after the incident. Her father describes her resilience: "She actually emits strength for both her mother and me, seeing how well she is handling this. She's got tons of support from her friends, and she's a real strong character."[13]

Forging an Identity vs. Performing for an Audience

One of a teenager's jobs is to form his identity, and the process of integrating multiple selves, many of which contradict one other, isn't easy. As one of psychologist Madeline Levine's teenage patients eloquently put it, "I feel like a puzzle, only I can't get all the parts to fit."[14] There are worries that living a life online can make this job even harder. We know that teens experiment by assuming different online identities or pretending to be different ages.[15] They can also forge different versions of themselves, on a minute-by-minute basis if they choose, through the photos they upload to Facebook or the musings they post on blogs. MIT professor Sherry Turkle worries that the selves our teens are creating this way are designed for public consumption, so young people play to the audience. The identities that result from this process are externally manufactured rather than internally developed, "so those moments in which you're supposed to be showing your true self become a performance."[16]

However, it could equally be argued that through exercises such as blogging and creating personal websites, teenagers are practising using words and images to shape their own authentic narratives, and learning how to decipher and interpret their own stories. In *Say Everything*, Scott Rosenberg talks about a Web designer who was able to bolster her confidence in her own ideas and gain self-awareness from posting her ideas online. She found that the daily exercise helped her discover her true interests. "Where did all these links to archaeology articles come from? Oh, right, she'd actually been interested in the subject as a child, but had never pursued it."[17] By re-examining her life through the decisions she was making online, she was able to discover some life themes. Also, since search engines both aggregate and reveal our teens' multiple selves, they make it harder for our teens to live separate identities. When it is easy to google a name and find that the belly dancer and the choir singer are the same person, our teens are forced to integrate, or at least acknowledge, their different puzzle pieces.

Parents play a significant role in supporting a teen's developing identity and it's important to be mindful of our impact. For example, family mythologies shape a teen's sense of self. The underlying themes may be openly acknowledged or subtly communicated, and understanding them can help us mediate the negative messages and support the positive ones. Families may define themselves as "hard workers" or "athletic," or more sadly as "losers" or "unlucky," and there may be multiple and even conflicting images depending on the visions of different family members. Within the family, individuals might be labelled "the smart one," "the creative one," "the athletic one," or they may be set up in opposition to one another, such as "the good one" and "the bad one." Then there are the labels that we all use to define ourselves, such as, "I can't do math" or "I'm bad at sports." And on it goes, with generalized and stereotyping descriptions that can become self-fulfilling, for better or worse.

We know the day-to-day language of the family is sending powerful messages because merely reading suggestive words can be sufficient to influence our actions. In *Blink*, Malcolm Gladwell describes a study in which a group of students were given a scrambled-sentence test that included words such as "aggressively," "bold" and "intrude." Thus, primed to be rude, they acted true to form in a subsequent encounter. Another group in the same circumstances acted politely after doing the same test sprinkled with words such as "respect," "considerate" and "courteous."[18]

Knowing the power of family mythology, my husband and I used storytelling to shore up our teens' sense of self and position them as part of a historical continuum. In *The Triumph of Narrative*, Robert Fulford writes that narrative is how we explain, how we teach and how we entertain ourselves. "Children grow into adults by learning stories, and so do nations and communities." He quotes the philosopher Alasdair MacIntyre, who warns, "Deprive children of stories and you leave them unscripted, anxious stutterers in their actions as in their words."[19] If your family history is like ours, many of the stories from the past seem boring at first glance. But it doesn't take much imagination (or exaggeration) to turn them into exciting tales with which to enthrall your teens while you're on a car trip or sitting around the campfire.

In our case we painted a vivid picture of our feisty, tenacious, never-say-die ancestors to inspire our daughters with the strength of their genetic inheritance. They were lucky enough to hear first-hand accounts from their grandparents about the hard work and courage that underlay their successes. When it came to their maternal Scottish lineage, I explained that our clan was unique in having a female chief, a formidable woman who led the clan for half a century, and that the family motto *Fortis et Fidus* (strong and loyal) succinctly captured the clan traits. By embellishing our genealogy a tad I created a "Warrior Woman" ancestry of the imagination. When my daughters were in their late teens we took a family pilgrimage to explore these Scottish roots, including a visit to the clan chief and the castle ruins, and we tracked down where our ancestors lived before leaving for Canada in the mid-1800s. From time to time I've worried that I've laid it on a bit thick, especially the part about "loyalty," and I've tempered the rose-coloured tales with examples of the downsides of blind devotion using stories from both Scottish history and their own teenage lives.

Rohini took her two teenage sons on a similar voyage of family mythology, leaving their New York home to spend five weeks in India and explore their grandparents' roots.

"The city we stayed in, Chennai, has a rich history going back to the first century A.D.," Rohini explains, "and it produced some of the greatest minds and most successful people of the world. I made sure the boys got to do many things around historic sites, exploring age-old architecture from various eras. I took them to centuries-old temples and to the beach, and to restaurants with mouth-watering Tamil food. One real plus was finding a playground where young boys were playing cricket. After watching them play, I found them cricket bats and balls, and badminton racquets and feather shuttlecocks. They loved these new sports and played them to their hearts' content with the new friends they made in the neighbourhood. I was happy that I got to share our cultural heritage with my sons, and to this day they remember the trip with nostalgia. It was fun to see them brag to their friends about all their discoveries when they returned. It turned out to be one of the most wonderful experiences of my life, despite the many difficulties I encountered as a mother who tried to accomplish a bit too much on a single trip!"

There are lots of ways to create your family mythology that don't require visiting the ancestral lands. My friend is from Columbia and her husband is from Greece and they wanted their daughter to understand the richness of both heritages. By living in a Greek section of the city, with its restaurants, stores and local residents, they absorb the sounds and colours of Greece every day. To bring the Latin American side of their culture alive, they take in young boarders, mainly from Columbia and Mexico, who stay with them for months at a time to attend an English-language school. You could mistake their kitchen for its Latino counterpart with its food, music and dancing. Their daughter revels in the strengths (and the challenges) of her family mythology and its dual cultures.

While acknowledging the value of family mythology in supporting the creation of self, we need to be conscious of another fine line. We don't want our positive images to deteriorate into unrealistic pressure or rigid parental expectations. Phrases such as "our family has always excelled academically" or "for generations we've been lawyers and you'll be one too" are likely to interfere with our teen's healthy development of self. Madeline Levine treats lots of teens whose parents are over-involved in how well their children perform. In *The Price of Privilege*, she says our goal should be to help our children develop skills that will lead them to set their *own* bar high and support them to see the world through their own eyes without being afraid of disappointing us. Psychoanalyst Carl Jung put the problem succinctly when he said, "The greatest burden a child must bear is the unlived life of the parents."

Mentors can act as role models to help our teen shape her identity. As a teenager I remember deliberately identifying a couple of older counsellors at camp whom I wanted to grow up to be like. I remember thinking that they were "strong and smart—but sexy," which, for a female in the fifties, was still a contradiction in terms. Christy Haubegger, founder of the magazine *Latina*, had several mentors when she was a teenager—her mother, her brother and a lawyer she worked for during her last year of high school. "Each person gave me something different: my mother modelled true strength and was a living example of a working mom who managed to balance home and work life; my brother (my primary playmate for many years) taught me, albeit unknowingly, that I could do anything a boy could do (as evidenced by my scraped knees); and my employer trusted me and believed I was smart and ultimately convinced me that it was within my reach to pursue a law career if I chose to. These people each taught me certain values, and I was able to pick and choose from each of them. The perfect person who models all character traits will seldom come your way (who is perfect, after all?), but if you can develop your own 'composite' mentor, so to speak, you are free to admire the strengths of each unique individual and absorb them."[20]

One of the most significant mentors for our daughters has been the nanny whom we hired when the children were infants. Well over two decades later, Ofelia remains an integral part of our family. She extends boundless love and caring to those around her and sets high expectations that our daughters should reciprocate in kind. When my daughter was fourteen, she and a friend tricked Ofelia into authorizing their borrowing of some restricted movies. When the ruse was discovered, Ofelia was hurt and embarrassed. Both girls, with tears in their eyes, apologized for misleading her and swore they would never do it again. She forgave them. They have kept their promise and learned a powerful lesson at her knee. Another of Ofelia's contributions to their character development comes from her irrepressible sense of humour. From day one she has teased them about their little foibles and made them laugh at life's circumstances. While we parents were maybe a tad too precious with our daughters' feelings, she was masterful at getting them to loosen up and get over themselves. They will live their lives with a lighter spirit and a deeper sense of caring, thanks to her.

The most overt clashes between parents and a teen's emerging identity revolve around appearance. Here's Eleanor's advice: If it is not illegal, immoral or hurtful, let it go. "My son Ron has dreadlocks," she says, "so people sometimes treat him like a stoner. But he can handle it. He likes himself; it's his identity." When Helen talks with her teenagers about the way they look she's careful to focus on what's appropriate, rather than criticizing their style. "The negotiation is not about what *I* want," she says, "for example, 'no son or daughter of mine is going to . . . ,' but rather 'have you really thought this through, and are you aware that. . . .'" At the same time, Helen knows they need to develop their own style. "I certainly had *my* own style as a teenager—much to the chagrin of my parents—big oversized glasses, a shaved multicoloured head, a red silk dress and beige suede pumps. I shudder at the thought now, but I thought I looked fabulous!"

Some parents are determined to do things differently because they remember the criticism they received in their teenage years. "When I was a teenager," Carol says, "I received a steady stream of criticism cloaked as advice. I think my mother genuinely intended it as fashion tips, but I heard it as criticism. So comments about how vertical stripes were more flattering, or how V-neck sweaters accentuated this or that, made me very self-conscious and embarrassed about my appearance. As a result, I have tried very hard to avoid any of this with my daughters. When one of my daughters became heavy, I made no reference, and when they choose clothes that look terrible, I try to keep my mouth shut (and *usually* succeed)."

Debbie took the same approach with her sons. "I didn't love all their clothes, especially the five or so years when their oversized pants hung low on their hips, with the crotch approaching the knees. But this was 'the look' they chose, and I never said a word. Shopping expeditions were always fun, and I made a big deal out of it when they looked sharp within the confines of 'the look' they'd chosen. They couldn't hear too many times how good, how cool, how handsome they looked."

My mother's reaction to my hair when I was a teenager helped me accept my daughters' many and varied hair-styles and colours during their teenage years. At the age of fourteen, I came home from camp with orange hair, having achieved this desired effect by pouring peroxide on my head and sitting in the sun for hours. My friends' mothers were horrified, and assumed my mother would force me to go back to my natural colour. But my mother said, "It's only hair." More importantly, she said, "Since you want to change your hair colour, I'll pay for you to have it done properly—once." So after that one expensive procedure, which gave it a more attractive hue, I figured out how to maintain my hair myself with cheap off-the-shelf products. My mom's support and acceptance meant a great deal to me. So when my daughters created wild hair colours from a variety of do-it-yourself products, they would pay for the dye themselves, but I paid for them to have their hair cut professionally.

My reasoning was that, regardless of hair colour, a good haircut automatically moved a teenager from the category of "disaffected punk" to "creative art student." My hope was that this more socially acceptable image would generate a more positive response from the casual observer, whether store clerk or passerby, and my daughters would be treated better, and feel better about themselves. The public reaction to my daughters usually proved me right. One memorable incident took place when I was with my daughter at a local food store during her spiky-pink-hair phase. An elderly, conservatively dressed woman came right up to her face and said in a loud voice, "I saw your hair, and I thought, 'What is that girl thinking?'" She then paused for a deep intake of breath. Standing some distance away, I prayed fervently that my daughter would hold her tongue. Everyone had now turned to look, and the woman continued in full voice, "And, you know what—I think you look *terrific!*"

But Sherry Turkle's concern that the Internet is making our teens too externally focused is a good reminder of the genuine danger in being too dependent on praise from the audience. I remember my mother's wise words when, as a teen, I was agonizing over some peer rejection. Although the nature of the slight is long forgotten, I remember well what she said: "Her opinion seems so important to you now, but, soon, she won't be a part of your life. In a few years you won't even remember her name. If you make life decisions to seek her approval, soon she'll be long gone and you'll be the one stuck with the choices." This struck me as an extraordinary piece of insight, and I repeated the words "soon I won't even remember your name" like a mantra for many years, whenever I faced unwelcome peer pressure. Years later, when my daughters came to me with similar problems, I was glad to have this response ready at hand.

Real Friends vs. Virtual Friends

With our teens spending so much time online, we worry that virtual friends are replacing their real friends, and that these virtual friends may prove dangerous. Our anxieties are heightened by reported cases of Internet seduction or "grooming," the technique used by a sexual predator to convince an underage person to have relations with them off-line. However, research conducted by the Pew Research Center found that only a very small number of teens report uncomfortable online contact and most of them handled the contact ably by deleting or ignoring it.[21] Research reported in *American Psychologist* found that those adolescents who are most at risk of Internet-initiated sex crimes often engaged in other risky behaviours and had difficulties in other parts of their lives. Their backgrounds included abuse, childhood trauma, rule-breaking behaviours, depression and social-interaction problems.[22]

To inoculate our teens against online predators, we need to help them recognize when they are being groomed and teach them not to respond and to alert us. And we need to impress upon them that if they really think they have to meet someone they met online in person, they must never go alone. The goal of WiredSafety is to keep kids and teens safe in cyberspace by providing them with expertise in safe, secure and responsible interactive technology use. The Q&A section for parents provides answers to the question "How can I tell if my child is communicating with an Internet predator?"

But for most teens, life online merges and overlaps with their off-line life and is an extension of, rather than a substitution for, the physical world. So the friends they see every day are the ones they chat with online. And the Internet has the added advantage of allowing teens to extend that circle beyond one close-knit group, and lets them easily stay in touch with other friends, including those who live nearby whom they don't bump into regularly, or those in different cities.[23]

Joan's daughter is in a specialized learning program and nearly 90 percent of the students in her high school are bussed from a wide geographic area. "Megan's friends are really scattered," Joan explains, "and she stays connected with them online. But the world of cyberfriends is broad and she also meets the friends of her friends. I frequently query her about their identities and get responses like, 'he plays hockey with Kevin' or 'she goes to youth group with Amanda.' Anyone she can't account for has to be 'unfriended.' As parents we need to ensure that proper safety precautions are taken if our child is meeting someone face to face whom we don't know. Recently, my daughter wanted to go to an amusement park with a boy she had met at camp several years previously, and with whom she had reconnected on Facebook. I made sure she went as part of a group. I was concerned for her safety, and, also, I wanted her to have someone with her in case the boy didn't show up, or in case they didn't get along after all these years."

Research shows that having extended friendship networks can support our children throughout the teen years by helping them withstand pressure from bullies, and by providing comfort if they fall out of favour for a time with any one group. "If a primary set of friends starts heading in a direction that makes them uncomfortable, they can save face by pleading commitments with their swim team friends or their summer camp friends," Carol explains. "This way, all their eggs are not in one basket." And since each set of peers has its own unique values and measures of success, if your child does not excel according to one group's criteria, she may find a niche somewhere else.

If you're worried that your teen is spending too much time with the same group of friends, either off-line or on, you might want to deliberately nurture relationships. Some mothers I know set out to offer an enrichment program for their daughters and ended up also providing them with a supportive peer group. Once a month for the past several years, about a dozen of them have taken turns organizing educational events for their daughters. The evenings have included a wide variety of topics, including sessions on leadership, women's history, African drumming and Italian cooking. When the group was initially set up, the girls all lived in the same neighbourhood and attended the same school, but over the years they have gone off in different directions. This monthly activity keeps them connected, and the group composition remains fluid so they can introduce new participants. Judging from the times I have seen this group in action, the young women feel safe to be themselves with one another, and they are empowering one another to develop into thoughtful, passionate and engaged young people.

Involvement in sports or the arts is another way for your teen to expand his networks. These activities, whether playing soccer, working on a mural, performing with a jazz combo or putting on a play, provide opportunities to make new friends and practise off-line social skills. And the strength of the friendships being forged in these activities can be significant. A recent study tracked the grades of hundreds of secondary school students over a three-year period and found that exam results could be predicted based on proficiency in the music class. The lead researcher concluded that one reason for this result was the socio-emotional benefits the students gained from being a part of the music class. "The quality of the relationships they develop in these classes are much better than the quality of relationships in other classes, and this is really important to high-school kids."[24]

When my daughters were young, a friend with teenage children advised me to make sure that my children had friends outside of school, whether from after-school activities, summer camps or the neighbourhood, and we made a real effort in this regard. When our daughter was in her last year of high school, she announced one day that she had figured out why she was coping well. She credited her multiple peer groups as one of the factors. Her school put a great deal of pressure on students to maintain high academic standards, and the pressure came not only from the teachers and administrators, but from other students. While some of the teens were able to handle the stress, others were seeing therapists and taking pills. Here's how our daughter summed up the reasons for her resilience: "I have activities outside school so I know there's life elsewhere. I didn't start this school in kindergarten like so many others, so I know all schools aren't like this. I know you and Dad will love me even if I don't get good marks. And my best friend keeps me sane, and she never lets me beat up on myself."

Another important way to add to your teen's storehouse of friends is through providing loving, meaningful relationships with adults other than their parents. In *Hold On to Your Kids*, Neufeld and Maté talk about the work of the psychologist Julius Segal, a pioneer of research into what makes young people resilient. Segal summarized studies from around the world and concluded that the most important factor in keeping children from being overwhelmed by stress was the presence in their lives of a charismatic adult, "a person with whom they identify and from whom they gather strength."[25]

Sometimes these relationships just happen, but often they need to be encouraged. The adult could be a relative, a friend of yours, a neighbour, or your teen's employer. The parents of your children's friends can be another great source of support, and your teen can benefit from the unique strengths of these families. My daughter's best friend had a Columbian mother and Greek father, and they called her their "second daughter." The Latino atmosphere my daughter absorbed in this lively household, along with the language, music and food, was an excellent antidote to our calm, sedate WASP home. It has made her a better linguist, dancer and appreciator of cultural differences.

You can encourage these relationships by setting up opportunities for your teenager to interact with caring adults by hosting neighbourhood get-togethers or dinner parties with friends. For a decade, all through our daughters' teen years, we held an annual holiday brunch to which we invited dozens of families. Through this event, and other gatherings at our home, the girls practised having conversations with older people and developed friendships with several of them. A few have become important mentors to our daughters as they have selected schools, chosen courses of study and considered career paths. These relationships have offered the gifts of expert advice, ongoing support and unconditional love.

If your teenagers are lucky, their grandparents are a positive force in their lives, and the Internet can facilitate these connections, as we know from the earlier example of Frances Kaplan web-chatting with her teenage grandsons. Author Mary Piper says that it was the time she spent with her grandmothers that saved her when she was going through periods of hating her body, her town and her school.[26] Wilma Mankiller, the first woman chief of the Cherokee Nation of Oklahoma, also credits her grandmother with helping her feel better about herself. "Even though she was strict, she was never judgemental. At a very critical point in my life, she helped me learn to accept myself and to confront my problems."[27] My friend recalls a time when her teenage nephew was having a tough time at home and didn't seem to be able to get along with anyone. She was amazed when he moved in with his grandparents. "I remember thinking they had a lot of courage to take him in, especially at their age, because he was really troubled. But it worked out somehow, and was just what he needed."

By surrounding your teen with caring adults you increase the odds they will have someone to turn to if they are struggling with a friendship, whether real or virtual. When my fourteen-year-old friend was determined to go to a concert with a fourteen-year-old boy she had met online, she asked for my help. The two young people had been communicating via Skype for many months and, although they lived in different cities and had never met face to face, she told me he was her "closest friend." With the agreement of her parents I arranged a meeting at my house with my young friend, the boy and the boy's mother. We all passed one another's inspection and the two young people attended the concert together. They were completely satisfied with the evening, even though adult accompaniment was part of the deal. This was several years ago and the two have remained close friends. Looking back, my friend recognizes that the relationship supported and sustained her through a very rough patch in her life, and is grateful we facilitated it.

Privacy vs. Anonymity

One of the fuzziest lines in the digital world lies between our legitimate concern for personal privacy and the potential downsides of anonymous behaviour. As a start, we need to remind our teens that in this day and age they shouldn't do or say anything they wouldn't want known, because the odds are good that someone will find out. This has always been true in close-knit communities, and in that respect, the digital world is a small town. Jordan told me about four girls in his school who thought they could get away with creating a Facebook page that cruelly mocked other students by hiding behind an anonymous profile. Far from being safe from exposure, they were caught and suspended from school for cyberbullying.

And Stephanie told me this story. "I told a supposed friend my MSN password and she sent nasty messages to all my contacts pretending to be me. Luckily my sister, who was away at school, got one of the messages. She was completely shocked by it and called home right away, only to find out that I was away for the weekend and couldn't possibly have sent the message. My other sister got on my computer and figured out what had happened. She re-messaged everyone and changed my password. I learned a good lesson about keeping my password private and about what people do when they think they're anonymous."

It's not only young people who are trying to hide their bad behaviour in cyberspace. Author and historian Orlando Figes defamed the work of other authors in "anonymous" reviews on Amazon, while praising his own book. He was found out and had to pay damages and legal costs to the authors.[28] And then there are people whose behaviour gets digitally recorded by passersby. In a well-publicized case, a traveller at the Vancouver airport used his cellphone to record the tasering of Robert Dziekanski by the RCMP. The recording was played and replayed on television sets around the world and served as crucial evidence in provoking an inquiry into Dziekanski's death.[29] And then there are the daily screen captures of more minor deviances, like the photo my friend took the other day, using her cellphone to record some students misbehaving. She e-mailed the image to the principal of their high school and the students still don't know how the principal caught them.

On the privacy side, it's hard to keep up with the continual introduction of new hardware and software. With each new technology our teens need to figure out the privacy settings and there seem to be revelations about privacy breaches every day. Google was investigated for collecting personal information while gathering data for its Street View mapping service, and Facebook generated an onslaught of criticism when it tried to automatically share a user's profile details with the wider Web unless the user changed the default setting and opted out. I just found out that when I take a photo with my iPhone, coordinates are imbedded in the image that reveal precisely where the photo was taken. Evidently I can switch off the function, but I haven't done it yet, and I'm not sure I care.[30] But if what is being recorded is the location of my teen, maybe I should care.

It also appears that many iPhone apps secretly collect and transmit users' personal information. I may not mind that a third of all free iPhone apps try to access my geographic location, if I'm using one of them to identify the best nearby restaurants. But it turns out that some of those apps are trying to access my list of contacts, and that's worrisome. The problem seems to be that many app developers don't know how to verify whether the code they are using is malicious or not.[31]

Parry Aftab, executive director of WiredSafety, says that the most important lesson she can teach parents is how young people can innocently give out information online and how easily strangers can get this information. This happens when teens post personal profiles, complete online contest or registration forms, build a website, or forget to set their privacy settings. (See Aftab's safety guide for parents at the Wired Kids, Inc. website [see p. 262 for the URL].)

If it's any consolation, older teens appear to be more judicious about these privacy issues than we adults. A recent

Pew study found that eighteen- to twenty-nine-year-olds are more concerned about their online profiles than older adults, and they more actively manage their personal information. For example, nearly three-quarters of younger users have altered their privacy settings on social networks, as opposed to just over half of users older than fifty. More of the younger users have deleted unwanted comments that others have made about them and removed their names from photos. (We might argue they have more reason for doing so, but that's another issue.) They are also generally less trusting of the sites that host their content than older people.[32]

Ginny is seventeen and says that by the time you reach your teen years you've had issues about personal privacy drilled into you in media class. "We've been learning since we were kids never to go on webcams with people we don't know, and not to give out information to people we don't know. We always share scary stories about abductions from online perverts. They get passed around in chain mail." So, although we shouldn't let down our guard, it is reassuring that our teens seem to be looking out for each other.

One technique that teens are using to protect their privacy is to designate certain sections of their site accessible only to certain people, so that their mother and their boyfriend don't have to inhabit the same space. Helen was initially concerned when she found out that her daughter had created a new Facebook account using an alias that only a few friends knew. As her daughter explained, "You were the one who told me I should worry about future employers finding my photos. This way they can't." Helen will probably feel better knowing that a columnist for the *New York Times* admits having two separate Facebook accounts, one using her work name and one using her personal name. She did this so that her boss and publicists wouldn't be looking at her vacation photos. However, by revealing both user names in her article, she has blown her own cover and her colleagues may ask to befriend her alter ego.[33]

Sexual Well-being vs. Sexual Health

Maria has raised four children and feels that the pressure on young people to have sex has really accelerated. "There seems to be an expectation now among young teens that having sex is what you do," she says. "Many of my fifteen-year-old daughter's friends who are 'good girls' have had sex, and to add to my chagrin, some with multiple partners. I have heard many stories about 'couplings' at parties by teens who are not in relationships. One of my daughter's friends who has issues with self-esteem concluded it would be 'pathetic to be a seventeen-year-old virgin.' She's decided that if she hasn't lost her virginity by age seventeen, she will find someone, anyone, who will sleep with her. My daughter is trying to convince her to place a higher value on herself."

Research conducted at the Case Western Reserve University found that high-school students who spent the most time texting and on social-networking sites were more likely to engage in risky sexual behaviour. Nearly a fifth of the teens in the survey were "hyper-texters," defined as texting more than 120 messages per school day, and these hyper-texters were nearly three-and-a-half times more likely to have had sex and 90 percent more likely to report four or more sexual partners. These teens were predominantly female, lower socio-economic status, from a cultural minority and had no father in the home. While the researchers concluded that while texting did not necessarily cause this behaviour, it made it easier for the teens to work too hard to fit in. As the lead researcher explained, "If they're working that hard to fit in through their social networks, they're also trying to fit in through other behaviours they perceive as popular."[34]

Through the teen years my daughters found that, for the girls anyway, issues around sex were deeply connected with self-respect. In their early teens I remember them coming home after sex education classes and reporting being "grossed out" by the graphic images of sexually transmitted diseases. But as they grew older, it was the emotional toll of casual sex that concerned them more. My daughter was so distressed by the casual way in which a friend devalued herself when it came to sex that she put this quote from Janis Joplin on her dorm wall: "Don't compromise yourself, you're all you've got." Research findings show that my daughter was on the right track in her support for her friend. Particularly for teenage girls, a positive self-concept protects against risky sexual behaviour, including unprotected sex.[35]

The website It's a Teen's World (see p. 262 for the URL) has a quiz for teens that sheds light on the pressures today's hyper-sexualized world places on them to engage in sexual behaviour. The true/false questionnaire includes the statements "A lot of famous and rich people make sex tapes, post nude photos or send them to others (sexting), so it must be cool" and "Being slutty or acting like a 'player' is the way to be popular and cool." The Toronto documentary filmmaker Lynn Glazier set up the website to accompany her 2009 film *It's a Teen's World: Wired for Sex, Lies and Power Trips*, which asks teens about the price they pay to be cool, hip and popular in a sexually charged social world. Glazier says: "Kids today are growing up on a steady diet of reality TV that's far from real and that pushes sexual stereotypes—raunchy music videos, porn on the Internet, the clothing industry pushing everything skimpy, young stars behaving badly—and it has an impact on the way they relate to each other."[36]

The books our teens are reading aren't helping. Naomi Wolf, author of *Promiscuities*, reviewed a number of bestselling books aimed at teenage girls in the *New York Times Book Review*[37] and found the novels contained lots of sex, but not many healthy sexual relationships. The sex was all of a kind that Wolf describes as "blasé and entirely commodified." She feels that the novels reproduce the daily experience of teenage girls where "they are expected to compete with pornography, but still can be labelled sluts." Wolf's article was accompanied by a terrific list of alternative reading for teenage girls compiled by Justine Henning, founder of a website that recommends books for younger readers. Henning explains that some of the dozen books included in her list also contain fairly explicit passages relating to sex and/or drugs, but the context is different. She says, "As a parent and teacher, I only worry about that kind of content if it's presented in a morally irresponsible fashion which actively promotes dangerous behaviour."[38] You can access Henning's *New York Times* book list as a link under "About us" on her site (see p. 262 for the URL). The site also contains its own list of recommended books for teens.

We certainly get the impression that our teens are becoming more sexual, but the research says we're wrong, at least when it comes to the last fifteen years. A study that has been tracking teens since the mid-nineties found that little has changed in terms of their attitudes towards sex or when they first have sex. The research also found that the teens who are hooking up for casual sex are more likely to have lower grades and more school-related problems. Those teens who are having sex as part of a committed relationship do as well in school as students who are abstaining. The speculation is that serious relationships support school performance by providing social and emotional support and reducing stress.[39] What this says to me is that parents have a critical role to play in helping our teens develop an emotionally healthy and morally responsible attitude towards sexual relations.

Melody's sons are two-and-a-half years apart in age, and she found she never lacked for opportunities to talk with them about sex. "'Safe sex' was something with which my sons' generation grew up," she says, "so I didn't have to worry about passing on this lesson. But I was shocked when they started telling me jokes they picked up about gay sex, so I launched into the conversation about sexuality, choice, acceptance and love. I forbade them to call anyone a fag or gay in a derogatory way, and explained they could be inadvertently hurting a dear friend who was gay and wasn't prepared to share it yet. When a friend's brother died of AIDS, he left a letter to be read at his memorial service about his life as a homosexual. I read this letter to them, and we all wept at the suffering he had endured before coming out. I always presented sex as lovemaking to my sons, and made it clear that for me, love and sex were difficult, if not impossible, to separate. So I wanted them to always consider their own feelings, as well as their partner's, before having sex."

At age fourteen, one of Helen's daughters became sexually involved with another teen. "When we found out, we wanted to convince her to stop," Helen says, "but we knew fear-mongering wasn't going to work. So I tried to come up with a powerful, alternative image. I told her the story of her birth and what a truly magical event it had been for us. Because we were completely ready for the moment, her birth had been one of the happiest moments of our lives. I said, 'This is what I want for you, and, more importantly, this is what you should want for yourself.' The vivid image of 'what should be' convinced her to end the relationship. When it comes to the sex lives of my teenagers, I've found that drawing them towards an ideal has worked better than scare tactics and negative messages." Although using Helen's strategy may not convince older teens to give up sex, it may draw them towards more positive sexual relationships.

Sharon Hersh wrote *"Mom, Sex Is No Big Deal!"* for mothers. The goal was to help them become their daughter's ally in developing a healthy sexual identity. The author calls her book a "crash course in how to talk with our daughters about sex."[40] She reminds us that as mothers we may not be able to have any impact on society's glorification of sexual activity, but we can have a profound impact on our daughter. The book outlines the steps to follow in tackling the subject, beginning with understanding your daughter's world and your own sexuality, and then building bridges between the two worlds. There are sections on abusive dating relationships, addictive dating relationships and questions regarding sexual orientation.

When Carol sensed that her daughter was engaging in promiscuous behaviour with some of the boys at her school, she decided to use the indirect approach. "I told my daughter that I had recently run into an old friend from my high-school days. I said that I recalled this friend having a difficult time at one point because she began engaging in certain sexual activity with a few boys, making her suddenly very much in demand by many boys. I said, 'And suddenly she had popularity and a reputation based only on sex, and it took her years to find friends who were really her friends.' My daughter's eyes were wide open with surprise, and maybe recognition. I think the story hit home."

Several parents raised the "mixed sleepover" as an issue they had to face. This activity is portrayed by teens as a wholesome event where young men and women hang out together all night watching videos and playing games. And yes, my daughters assure me that some sleepovers are exactly as advertised—but others turn out differently. A friend told me about one that took place at his house. Despite his best efforts at supervision, he found out in the morning that his son had had sexual relations for the first time with his girlfriend. Since both of them were underage, and it had happened under his watch, my friend said he felt duty-bound to tell the girl's parents. The fallout was terrible for everyone, and my friend's son complained bitterly that the girl never spoke to him again.

Carol says that when her fourteen-year-old daughter asked if she could have a sleepover, she was completely caught off guard. "I said, 'Sure, with whom?' expecting to hear the name of a girlfriend," she remembers. "When she replied, 'Darryl,' my jaw dropped and I tripped over my words. I finally recovered enough to suggest that Darryl would be welcome to stay over, and that the den would be free that night for his use. A lengthy discussion ensued about how I should see this like any other sleepover, and why was I reading sexual activity into the equation. And then my daughter came up with the ultimate charge designed to hit home with me. 'I'm shocked that an open-minded and innovative person like you would be so traditional!' In the end, Darryl did not come for a sleepover. It turned out he was busy with something else, anyway. I just wish I had been ready for this one, and done some advance thinking. I might have had the same response, but I wouldn't have felt so ill-prepared for the debate."

If you'd like some help with your teen's sexual health, cyberspace has lots of resources. One interesting example is "Teens talking to teens about sex," a program run by Planned Parenthood Toronto, which uses instant messaging (IM), phone and e-mail to let teens talk to other teens who have been trained to answer their questions about sex and sexuality. Their website (see p. 262 for the URL) discusses such topics as sexual readiness, the changes of puberty, losing your virginity and the different stages of relationships in intelligent, non-hysterical language. All communication is strictly confidential.

The project's emphasis on personal privacy is well founded, since research shows that adolescents are more likely to use reproductive-health services when confidentiality is assured, and when they perceive the services as specific, sensitive and responsive to their needs.[41] When my daughters entered their teens, I wanted them to have an independent source of medical advice—someone with whom they could raise medical concerns, especially issues around sex, in confidence. So I arranged for them to become patients at a clinic staffed by young female doctors. I knew my own doctor would have respected their patient confidentiality, but it was a matter of perception. Also, I wanted to emphasize that they were responsible for their own bodies. Interestingly, my daughter now reports that she prefers male doctors because she has found them to be less judgemental.

We know that teens are worried about the health consequences of their sexual activity. When young people were asked to rank their concerns about mental health and wellness, sexually transmitted diseases (STDs) and HIV/AIDS were right at the top, with unplanned pregnancy not far behind.[42] *Adventures In Sex City*, a web-based sexual-health promotion game developed by a team of young people aged fifteen to twenty-one, lets our teens get the facts in private. In the game, four Sex Squad Superheroes set out to defeat the infected Sperminator and, in the process, the player gets reliable information on STDs. The game developers wanted to create something for youth that would give them the facts about sex but in a way that was daring and exciting. A sixteen-year-old named Genevieve reviewed the game on YouTube. "I loved it. I learnt a lot. The best part is you answer these questions and if you get it wrong, you learn from your mistakes . . . you are learning from a game, not in real life." The game is available from the website of the Middlesex-London Health Unit.[43] Another resource is the website www.kidshealth.org, which offers a comprehensive section on sexual health aimed at teenagers. The site offers answers, advice and straight talk, covering everything from puberty and menstruation to infections.

The Teen Spirit

Real Life vs. Virtual Life

WHEN novelist and screenwriter Michael Ventura was teaching a graduate writing seminar he was astonished when two of the brightest students in his class insisted they could go to Rome via a computer program and have as "real" an experience as if they'd actually been there. Ventura protested that this one-dimensional experience could never include the "unprogrammed." As he said, "James Baldwin's truth that 'any human touch can change you' isn't available on your computer."[1] But he admits that his arguments left his students unconvinced.[2]

Living a virtual life can be very seductive for our teens, so we need to work hard to keep them connected, both to us and to the real world. It's all too easy for today's teens to slip into a parallel universe with minimal overlap with the rest of the family. This was true even before the Internet, but the cyberworld our teens inhabit has made escaping reality child's play. As our teen is sitting next to us, she may be texting a friend, blogging on her website, playing a game, downloading music and movies or updating her Facebook page. (Oh, and maybe doing school work!) You used to be able to plop down next to your teen on the sofa while he was watching television; now he's more likely to be watching the TV show on his laptop. Since many teens have their own computer, they don't even have to negotiate with other family members to share the machine. And then, if you do ask her to unhook from the tether of the computer, she can put in her earbuds and retreat to her music. If you are trying to track down your teen, you can call him on his cellphone, but call display gives him a heads up, so he may decide not to answer. You can send off a text message to bypass this barrier, but you may not get a response, and you can't be positive that your message was received or read. All told, parents have to work very hard at maintaining an attachment to their teenagers.[3]

But we must stay connected to our teenagers, or suffer the consequences. Psychologist Madeline Levine finds that today's youth, whether they're in inner-city ghettos or exclusive gated communities, feel both physically and psychologically isolated from their parents. She links this isolation with an increase in depression, suicide and other psychological problems that compromise well-being.[4] In *Hold On to Your Kids*, Neufeld and Maté cite research confirming that the best protection for a teen is a strong attachment with their parents. "The primary finding was that teenagers with strong emotional ties to their parents were much less likely to exhibit drug and alcohol problems, attempt suicide, or engage in violent behaviour and early sexual activity."[5]

It was at a dinner party during my maternity leave where I first heard about the amount of attention teenagers require. I had just given birth to my first-born and was complaining to the woman sitting next to me that my leave wasn't long enough. I figured I should be spending more time with my daughter now, when she really needed me, and then I could get back to work. My companion's reply took me aback. "I continued to work full time when my children were young," she said. "It was when they became teenagers that I quit work and stayed home." Somehow I had imagined my children would need me less, not more, by the teenage years. As I subsequently found out, the problem isn't so much the amount of time that teenagers require—it's that you need to be available on *their* schedule—which is completely unpredictable.

As Hannah puts it, "The whole thing about teenagers is that ninety percent of the time what you're doing is just maintenance, like making sure they get fed. But every once in a while they need you, and at that moment when they need you, you have to be there, you have to have the right look on your face and you have to be completely available. So it's a question of always being ready if needed, but, hopefully, not to be needed."

One of the big problems is that we're often not awake when our teenager is in a mood to talk. My friend went through a period when she was worried about her teenage son's state of mind. She began taking naps in the early evening so she would be able to stay up and talk to him once he rolled home in the wee hours of the morning. During those late-night gabfests they talked about everything under the sun, and she is convinced those conversations were what saw him through a rough patch. "At least," she says, "they kept *me* from going insane with worry!"

Helen reminds us that it's not always easy to know when our teenagers need us, because they're not always sure themselves. "My husband and I were supposed to go to a party," she says, "but my daughter, Sharon, was in tears over an insult from a schoolmate, so I decided to stay home and comfort her. Sharon had presented a brave face to her dad, so he was convinced I was completely overreacting. I got some pressure from him to change my mind, but I was glad I put Sharon's needs first. It gave me a chance to really figure out what was going on, which, it turned out, had more to do with the way she felt about herself than anything to do with the schoolmate. If you miss the train on this one, you may miss one of those rare golden chances to really unearth some gem of understanding. Providing an emotional harbour for your children means having to change course when the warning bells sound."

One strategy for maintaining a real-world connection is to keep the family physically together when they're home, even if they're on their own screens. Debbie says, "When our kids were entering the teenage years, we tried to work against anything that would aide and abet them isolating themselves from the family. We resisted 'teen lines,' or TVs, VCRs and phones for their rooms (or later, cellphones) because we wanted to keep as much old-fashioned communal living alive as possible. The constant ringing of the telephone nearly drove us crazy, but at least we knew who was calling, and they weren't holed up in their bedrooms. We had one portable phone, so they could take that away for privacy." Emily's family made a similar decision to relocate technologies into a family space after realizing how much time her two teenage sons were spending squirreled away on their own. "We decided to curb the isolationist tendencies of our boys and reduce their 'screen time' by moving all the televisions, computers and Xbox games into common areas, and out of the basement and the boys' bedrooms." My friend admired her neighbours' ritual of "tea time," when the family would gather in the late afternoon in their smallish living room. "They loved crowding in with their kids and spending maybe thirty minutes catching up on the day with no interruptions."

Although the difficulties of staying connected hold true for both genders, they seem to be particularly acute with teenage boys. One young man told me that his teenage years were pretty "issue free" except that he felt his parents favoured his sisters. He speculated that the reason for this was that his sisters talked to his parents, whereas he never did. Looking back, he thinks that his parents were probably more anxious when it came to him, since they never knew what was going on. Upon reflection, he wasn't sure there was anything his parents could have done to make him more communicative.

In their book *Why Boys Don't Talk and Why It Matters*, Susan Morris Shaffer and Linda Perlman Gordon suggest a number of strategies parents can try. They say that boys don't naturally understand the importance of communicating their emotions, and that you have to teach them the language of feelings. They encourage parents to model empathetic behaviour by discussing their own feelings with their sons. My daughter remembers this strategy from our household and says, "You were always making us put our emotions into words."

Shaffer and Gordon also recommend small conversations instead of extended discussions or lectures, and say you should avoid interrogation. Emily uses this approach with her sons. "Asking direct questions such as, 'How was your day?' or 'Is something bothering you?' never works for me," she says. "Sometimes open-ended questions, such as 'What are kids at your school saying about all the newspaper discussion of oral sex?' or sharing my own *genuine* moral dilemmas has led to important conversations. I try to take advantage of windows of opportunity—a flurry of media interest in teenage sex, a teen acquaintance arrested for dealing drugs, an adult friend dealing with AIDS and homophobia, or an adult friend who is battling alcoholism—to discuss these issues. It tables our values and expectations with the boys, and keeps us connected."

Having stressed the difficulties some teenage boys have with communicating, I need to emphasize the dangers of falling into gender stereotyping on this issue. One of our challenges as a society is to continually affirm to our young men that being open, nurturing and engaged with people is masculine. Many girls can be equally remote and hard-to-reach during the teenage years, and many of the strategies recommended for connecting with boys can be just as useful for them.

The virtual world offers no physical contact so it's really important that we keep hugging our teens. This may seem hard to pull off when they're in a "don't-touch-me" phase, but we need to be persistent. When it came to her daughters, Carol found that offering massages was the trick. "I found that bedtime backrubs or anytime neck massages were always accepted, even when hugs, or even casual conversation, were not."

Debbie, the mother of two boys, is grateful a friend told her that teenage boys like and need physical attention from their mothers. "For some reason, probably the way things were in my family, I thought that having boys meant there'd be a lack of physical contact in the teenage years. When the boys were young, we were very cuddly and affectionate, and I was surprised and glad when it didn't stop as they got into their teens. We had a habit of giving hugs, quite a few times a day, for no particular reason. When I'd come up behind them as they were sitting at the table I'd massage their shoulders, or kiss the tops of their heads, and I never got shrugged off. They liked it, and weren't the least bit embarrassed to be affectionate in front of their friends. Life is full of surprises, and this was a good one for me. Without my friend's advice, I might have felt constrained to give them more space when they became young men, when, in fact, they enjoyed the physical affection."

Debbie found that it was particularly important to her sons to have a physically affectionate relationship with their father. "Once, when our eldest was thirteen, his father, Ned, put his arms around him in the kitchen and gave him a hug. I saw on the child's face a look of absolute *rapture* and I told Ned about this. I said that I felt that his affection was ten times more important to a boy at this age than affection from me. So Ned started to give him big hugs and our son couldn't get enough of it. Often, it would degenerate into male who-can-squeeze-the-life-out-of-whom, but it didn't matter, he just gloried in it."

Having a dog is another technique to keep your teen connected to the real world. Virtual pets might also need to be fed and walked, but they can't lick you. When our daughter was eleven, she spent months lobbying for a dog. We finally caved in and bought Samantha, a yellow Labrador puppy, and she became an integral part of the teen years for both girls. Many times the girls would come home from school and rush by us, with barely a word of greeting, to embrace the dog. Dog and daughter would then lie entangled on the sofa until our daughter was ready to deal with the rest of us.

My favourite Sam story took place the day my daughter started a new high school. No one had assigned her a locker, and, worse, her guidance counsellor had no idea how to find her one. The school, gargantuan in size, had nearly three thousand students, and being "lockerless" was like being homeless. She came home after school and lay prone on the kitchen floor, mute with despair, her head buried in her arms. Sam immediately took up a position right next to her, stretched out the length of her body, placed a paw gently on the top of her head and looked up at us. The message was clear. "Do not bother this girl." They lay there for a very long time until my daughter was ready to face the world again. I wasn't surprised to read that a Canadian police force used a dog to comfort grief-stricken teens who were bereft over the murder of one of their friends. As the victim services coordinator explained, "It's very cathartic to pet a dog. Dogs are unconditional in their affection and they're completely non-judgemental."[6]

To make sure our teens don't lose their taste for the real world, we need to give them lots of opportunities to enjoy its riches of taste, smell and touch. But for these experiences to have their full impact, everyone, including the parents, has to disconnect from digital devices, and it's just as often we adults who have a hard time exercising self-control. Through the teen years we took trips with our daughters of every length that were mostly digital-free, or at least digital-restricted. They ranged from afternoon outings to art galleries to major expeditions of several weeks' duration, from urban outings to outdoor adventures. We also used every possible family combination, from all four of us together, to each child alone with each parent. The trips had to be sufficiently interesting to engage them, sometimes to spots they proposed themselves, and mainly to places where there was no chance of running into their friends, thus sparing them the embarrassment of being seen with their parents. I can only remember one time when there was real resistance to this family togetherness. I was longing to go on a Scottish pilgrimage to explore our family roots, but it was going to be a trip of several weeks and, from a teenager's perspective, it lacked excitement. Our fourteen-year-old dug in her heels and wanted to be left at home. She was reluctantly persuaded to join us when my husband took her aside and explained how important the trip was to me. The message was an important one: "Sometimes we have to make personal sacrifices out of love and consideration for someone else."

"The value of spending quality time with your teenagers can't be overestimated," says Debbie, "and when it came to our two boys, outdoor adventures were the ticket. From the time they were seven and nine, until they were thirteen and fifteen, we spent two weeks every year on a wilderness canoe trip. We were completely on our own and dependent on our own company, without any interruptions or distractions." Teenagers remember these "hanging out" times as some of the best they had with their parents: lots of comfortable silences, no third degrees, just being together. "Travel with our kids has created a shared realm of experience that glues us together," says Eleanor, "and gives us so much to talk about. At the dinner table, the conversation invariably turns to the great, funny and frantic times we have spent together."

These kinds of trips provide challenges and achievements that can't be replicated in the virtual world. My husband has a tradition of doing an annual adventure outing with his daughters—sometimes with both of them together, sometimes separately, depending on their availability. "One of the great benefits of these trips," he says, "is the sense of personal accomplishment they get from keeping up with their old man. I remember my daughter's elation after a grinding hike, when she finally reached the snowfield at the top of a mountain. Several times she wanted to quit, but I kept reminding her how much fun it would be to reach the snowfield and have a snowball fight in the middle of summer. Her joy was unbounded when she finally made it to the top, and she then turned around and slid down the snow pack on her behind." And then there are those times when you get to prove that you're smarter than Dad. "I was meeting my daughter in a city that was new to her," my husband recalls. "I recommended a quick route to our hotel from the train station where she was arriving, but she figured out a faster way on her own. Her satisfaction at bettering my idea was a delight to behold."

And when you're travelling, you can usually count on a looming danger or two that can better any virtual game. "Our daughter was fourteen," my husband recalls, "and we were exploring deep into the backcountry of the Rocky

Mountains. When we reached the end of the road we decided to park the car and explore a beautiful trout stream. After gathering what we needed from the car, my daughter locked the door and slammed it shut. Only then did she realize that our only car key was locked inside. She panicked. She immediately envisioned several days of walking to reach a place where we might find help. It was a great chance for me to sit down with her and calmly discuss our options. She came to the accurate conclusion that the cheapest and safest option was to smash one of the car's small side windows and reach in and open the door. I showed her how to do this safely and with minimum damage by using a rock wrapped in a towel. If we don't offer our teens these real experiences, their world becomes diminished. But we need to be fully present. I felt my daughter's wrath on a recent trip when I spent too much time on my BlackBerry. It was not what she was used to, and she really let me know!"

The *New York Times* recently reported on an expedition of scientists who spent a week in a remote area of southern Utah to do some river rafting, camping and hiking. They were on a mission to understand how a retreat into nature might reverse the effects of heavy use of digital devices. Two of the scientists, who study teenagers' compulsive use of cellphones, argue that heavy use of technology can inhibit deep thought and cause anxiety. They believe that getting into nature can help relieve the symptoms. Other scientists in the group are less convinced.[7] I recommend we draw our conclusions from those who are used to spending time in the great outdoors, like the naturalist John Muir. Here's

Muir's finding on the impact of nature: "Climb the mountains and get their good tidings. Nature's peace will flow into you as sunshine flows into trees. The winds will blow their own freshness into you, and the storms their energy, while cares will drop away from you like the leaves of Autumn."

Self-esteem vs. Narcissism

One of the charges laid against the online world is that it's making our young people narcissistic and self-absorbed. As the argument goes, all this social networking, blogging and Twittering has encouraged our young people to think, "It's all about me." When test results are compared over time, today's young people are scoring higher on personality traits like self-confidence, vanity and self-importance. The Narcissistic Personality Inventory, for one, has found a significant increase in its narcissism score in some college samples when it asks people to agree with statements like "I know that I am good because everybody keeps telling me so," "Modesty doesn't become me," and "I always know what I'm doing." You can take a version of the test at http://psychcentral.com/quizzes/narcissistic.htm.

As Hal Niedzviecki writes in his book *Hello, I'm Special*, individuality has become the new conformity for all of us, not just teens, and nonconformity is now the accepted norm in society. As Niedzviecki says, we are "obsessed with celebrating our individuality" as we hurtle down "Mount Me."[8] So we should not be surprised if our teens reflect our society. This societal trend to self-absorption is further augmented by our teen's own stage of development; it is normal for narcissism to peak in young adulthood. As researchers at the University of Illinois explain, narcissism in our young people is an "age-related developmental trend."[9]

So what does an "age-related developmental trend" feel like if you're an adolescent? As Mara Sidoli explains in her book *The Unfolding Self*, it's not easy for teens to integrate all the major changes that are occurring—both in their bodies and in their new experiences of life. Sidoli gives one of the best one-line descriptions I've read about what it feels like to be a teen: "Shifts from excited to depressed states, from impotence to omnipotence, from insecurity to arrogance, from extreme passivity to frantic activity, and so on, occur frequently, often to extreme degrees."[10]

If we find it hard to tell some days whether our teen is a narcissist or full of valuable self-esteem, we would be wise to take psychologist Madeline Levine's advice and concentrate on helping them develop self-efficacy, rather than self-esteem. Levine explains that the two traits often overlap but they are not the same thing, and self-efficacy is more likely than self-esteem to contribute to healthy emotional development. Self-efficacy is the belief that we can successfully impact our world and is associated with judgements of personal capability, whereas self-esteem is concerned with judgements of self-worth. Levine explains that this sense of agency, or self-efficacy, begins in infancy. Baby learns that when he shakes his baby rattle it makes a noise. Levine asks us to imagine what it would be like if baby didn't get to shake the rattle for himself, if instead, overzealous parents did it for him.[11] I would add that some of these parents might feel the need to accompany their shaking with "Baby, you're doing such a good job!"—just to make sure baby's self-esteem isn't damaged. By the time this child is a teen he may have developed a sense of self-esteem that bears little relation to academic, personal or interpersonal success. It would be healthier for our teens if they were allowed to develop self-efficacy, coming from a sense of personal control that is grounded in a sense of agency.

What complicates the issue is that Levine has found her teenage patients to be suffering from "maladaptive perfectionist striving" as a result of parental pressure to achieve. She explains, "When parents place an excessively high value on outstanding performance, children come to see anything less than perfection as failure."[12] So when our teens agree with a statement in the Narcissistic Personality Inventory such as, "I know that I am good because everybody keeps telling me so," they could be masking a fear of failure.

We need our teens to learn that failure is an essential component of success, and that, when they fail, *we* will be able to cope. Probably my biggest parenting challenge was resisting the desire to rush in and rescue my children every time I anticipated the wall into which they were about to crash. But every time I heard the triumph in my daughter's voice when she solved her own problem, I was reminded to hold back on being the big saviour.

One technique I used with my daughters was to have examples of the failures of famous people at the ready that I could pull out if faced with their anguish over a disappointment or a setback. Here are some of the stories I used, culled from a variety of sources—with no concern for accuracy!

- As the story goes, Fred Astaire, one of the world's all-time greatest dancers, had a framed piece of paper over his fireplace—the rejection he had received after an audition. It read: "Can't act. Can dance—a little."
- Winston Churchill, prime minister of Britain during the Second World War, was asked, "Sir Winston, what in your school experience best prepared you to lead Britain out of her darkest hour?" Here's what he replied: "It was the two years I spent at the same level in high school." "Did you fail?" "No. I had two opportunities to get it right. What Britain needed was not brilliance, but perseverance when things were going badly."
- Albert Einstein, the renowned mathematician and physicist, said, "It's not that I'm so smart, it's just that I stay with problems longer."
- The great inventor Thomas Edison had to be home-schooled because he was considered "slow" by his teachers. Here's how he looked at failure: "I have not failed. I've just found ten thousand ways that won't work."

I used stories as a way of encouraging our teens to talk about "failures" in a humorous way. We had a routine at evening meals that lasted for many years where each of us would tell a story about the best thing and the worst thing that had happened to us that day. I started the practice as a way of getting the girls to talk about their day in a way that would go beyond, Q: "How did things go today?" and A: "Fine." But I soon realized the practice had other great benefits, including helping them find the humour in disaster, and building their storytelling skills. They loved hearing about things that had gone wrong for me, and my tales of daily disasters debunked any myth around adult competency. In *Becoming Human*, Jean Vanier says that by acknowledging my problems, I was also connecting with my children. "Power and cleverness call forth admiration but also a certain separation, a sense of distance; we are reminded of who we are not, of what we cannot do. On the other hand, sharing weaknesses and needs calls us together into 'oneness.'"[13]

My daughter was probably practising self-efficacy when she turned her "boarding disaster" into a prize-winning story. A resort where she had been snowboarding was replacing an old T-bar ski lift with a fancy new quad lift and asked people to send in their memories of being hauled uphill the old-fashioned way. My daughter's story described how she lost control of her snowboard on the T-bar and smashed into a lift pole, not just once, but when she tried again. She makes it all sound hilarious, even though her injuries were painful enough to require medical assistance. And here is where more fun began. A ski patroller strapped her into a sled, skied the sled down to the first-aid building and positioned the sled right under the rim of the roof. As she told the story, "Suddenly I hear a sliding sound and BOOM all the snow on the roof comes off and lands right on top of me, still strapped to the sled. So you'll understand why I'm not going to miss the T-bar." Her tale of woe won her a T-shirt in the story competition.

When our teens use the online world to focus exclusively on shallow presentations of self, then narcissism can substitute for accomplishment and agency. But when my daughter posted her story recounting this embarrassing moment, she publicly acknowledged her less-than-perfect snowboarding skills. By laughing at herself in an entertaining way, she was able to get some gain for her pain and demonstrated that her self-esteem was strong enough to take a little bruising.

Empathy vs. Indifference

Another serious charge laid at the feet of the online world is that today's young people are less caring than previous generations. Researchers at the Institute for Social Research at the University of Michigan have been studying empathy over the last thirty years and found a big drop after the year 2000. "College kids today are about forty percent lower in empathy than their counterparts of twenty or thirty years ago, as measured by standard tests of this personality trait," says Sara Konrath, one of the researchers on the study. The students today were less likely to agree with statements such as "I sometimes try to understand my friends better by imagining how things look from their perspective" and "I often have tender, concerned feelings for people less fortunate than me."

Konrath and her colleagues will be exploring the reasons for these findings in future studies, but they have a number of theories. They speculate that the culprits include exposure to violence in video games, celebrity reality shows with their hyper-competitive atmosphere, the ease of having "friends" online who are easy to tune out, and a general increase in the pace of life that leaves young people too busy worrying about themselves and their own issues to have time to empathize with others.[14] I would add to this list the uncertain economy and hyper-competitive job market. There are other possibilities. In *The Shallows*, Nicholas Carr cites research to support the argument that you need a calm, attentive mind to feel empathy and compassion. He says the Internet, by diminishing our capacity for contemplation, reduces our capacity to feel these subtler emotions.

When it comes to teens, it's important to remember that a certain indifference to the needs of others goes with the territory. Brain scans done by the UCL Institute of Cognitive Neuroscience show that when teenagers consider a course of action, they, unlike adults, hardly use the area of the brain that is involved in thinking about other people's emotions.[15] They are not very good at seeing things from someone else's perspective, or deciding how they would feel in another person's shoes. But if the research is accurate, and our teen's inability to empathize is eroding even further then we have our work cut out for us. As parents our job is to help them develop those empathetic skills, and mediate any pulls towards indifference that come from the online world.

When our children were very young we established a practice of donating to charity every Thanksgiving. We told our daughters that this was a time to give thanks for our good fortune by choosing charities to support for the year. Before they had their own money, we allocated an amount for them to give to worthy causes of their choice. They could give the full amount to one organization or parcel it out to a number of groups. Their priorities changed over the years, and the selections were an interesting indication of what was on their minds.

Maria found that church offered good opportunities for community service for her teenagers. "My husband and I wanted to instill in our children an appreciation for what they have, as well as a sensitivity towards those who are less fortunate," she says. "As teenagers they worked at an 'Out of the Cold' program where they served breakfast and lunch to homeless people every Saturday. They got to know some of the regulars and, I think, became more empathetic from this experience."

Artistic programs have the potential to open the minds of our young people to the realities of others. My daughter found that theatre studies made her a more empathetic and compassionate person. "One of the critical elements taught in drama class," she explains, "is the importance of understanding your character's motivation. It is only when you get inside his or her head that you can develop a persuasive dramatic portrayal." She feels that her years performing in plays have helped her to be culturally sensitive in her work.

Our daughters were in a school system where they were required to contribute a minimum number of volunteer hours in order to graduate. Volunteering has given them wonderful opportunities to give back to the community, and has also led to paid work opportunities. One daughter's volunteer job one summer as an intern with an international non-profit organization resulted in a paid internship the following summer with an international agency. In addition, they have both volunteered in political campaigns and this seems to have contributed to a passion for civic issues—or at least an addiction to reading newspapers, coupled with a compulsion to write editorial comments directly on the newsprint!

If community service is not part of your school's curriculum, your teen may need some encouragement and guidance. Many young people say they don't volunteer because they have not been personally asked, or they don't know how to get involved.[16] There are many organizations that could stimulate your teen's thinking about community service and many of them have a very compelling online presence.

Youth Noise wants to empower young people to take action to make change in their lives and in the lives of other young people, both locally and globally. Their site includes discussion boards, blogs and ways to connect with others in the global network (see p. 263 for the URL). They discuss issues such as global warming, peace activism, antipoverty, youth homelessness and animal rights. There are practical tips and links to sites for taking action, whether that action is volunteering, donating or sending e-mails to officials.

The international child rights organization Free The Children is a network of young people that encourages other young people to take action to improve lives everywhere. The organization was founded in 1995 by then-twelve-year-old Craig Kielburger to fight child labour. It now has more than one million youth involved in programs in forty-five countries, including building schools, developing alternative-income projects, shipping medical supplies, and providing healthcare and community funding. The website (see p. 263 for the URL) provides details of many ways to get involved, from starting a "youth in action" group to volunteering overseas. The website www.metowe.com encourages young people to care and contribute, as well as engage in activities that support Free The Children.

Craig Kielburger and his brother Marc tell the story of "Alex the Apathetic," a fourteen-year-old whose engagement with social activism changed his life. According to the Kielburgers, over the seven years that Alex worked with Free The Children, this brooding, disaffected teen was transformed into a youth leader, organizing volunteer excursions to far-flung countries, facilitating leadership training around the world, and delivering speeches to tens of thousands of young people. The Kielburgers say that people shouldn't dismiss the contribution teens can make. Otherwise, "society reinforces feelings of insecurity and low self-esteem so frequently found in this age group."[17]

Volunteering may not be as transformative for every teen as it was for Alex but it can be a terrific way to broaden worldviews, get into the habit of giving back to the community and acquire insights into future careers. According to the research, many youth have found that their volunteer experience gave them new skills they were able to apply in the workplace. And they say that one of the things that motivated them to become a volunteer was the opportunity to explore their own strengths.[18] Parents report that community involvement has helped their children succeed both inside and outside the classroom.[19]

And then there are those daily opportunities where we get a chance to model empathetic behaviour. My daughter says she won't forget the day I intervened in an incident with complete strangers at the shopping mall. We were looking for a place to park when we noticed a man shoving a woman who was trying to get her baby out of a stroller and into a car. All three of them seemed to be travelling together. I rolled down the window and asked the woman if she wanted me to call the police, and said I wouldn't leave until she told me what she wanted to do. Another woman shopper then joined in, and stood nearby and repeated my words. As the man hurled insults at us, we kept ignoring him and focusing on the woman. The woman who was being manhandled thanked us, said she would be all right, and they drove off together. I can't claim this incident changed their relationship, but the woman did seem to gain strength from our concern and from the solidarity of complete strangers. My daughter remembers the incident as a powerful lesson about our duty to reach out to others.

Depressed vs. Chemically Imbalanced

It is normal for teens to have emotional ups and downs, and recognizing when professional help is needed can be a challenge. It is estimated that one in five teenagers will have a mood disorder, caused by a chemical imbalance in the brain, and early intervention can make a huge difference in the success of the treatment. If left untreated, other problems can emerge, including substance abuse, declining school performance, aggressive behaviour, social isolation and self-harm or suicide.

Health practitioners are concerned about the impact the online world can have on a teen's mental well-being, especially if he is suffers from attention problems. We know, for example, that periods of rest are critical to brain development and that playing video games late at night disrupts sleep patterns. And then there is the problem of isolation. When our teens are holed up in their rooms for hours on end, lost in cyberspace, it's hard to assess their state of mind. At the same time, people like Leonard Davidman, a professor of psychiatry at New York Medical College, wants to acknowledge the potential of the digital world to save teenagers' lives. He cites examples from his own practice when cellphones gave him emergency contact with his teen patients. "A teenager at risk for suicide is able to text me in the evening about a traumatic flashback," he says. "And a teenage patient in the midst of a classroom crisis, borrowing a friend's cellphone, texts me for an immediate urgent session, thus preventing a violent outburst."[20]

If your teen is experiencing more severe and longer-lasting mood swings that go beyond being "down in the dumps," it is important to seek help. Fortunately there are a number of resources available to help both you and your teen to assess the situation. Mind Zone (see p. 263 for the URL) is a mental-health website for teens sponsored by the Annenberg Foundation Trust with support from the University of Pennsylvania. Topics covered are anxiety, bipolar disorder, depression, eating disorders, schizophrenia and suicide. Information and advice is provided under three themes: cope (learning ways to manage), care (taking care of yourself) and deal (understanding the facts). All content has been reviewed by a psychiatrist specializing in child and adolescent care.

Check Up from the Neck Up (see p. 263 for the URL) offers a private online survey that allows people to assess their own mental health. After answering a series of questions, you receive feedback as to whether your answers suggested indicators for depression, bipolar disorder, panic disorder or generalized anxiety disorder. If you score a moderate or high probability for mood disorder, you are urged to see your family physician as a first step. You can print out the results and discuss them with your doctor.

The process is confidential and your results are erased from the server when you leave the website.

Mind Your Mind (see p. 263 for the URL) is a website for youth by youth on topics related to mental health and mental illness. The site offers information, resources and tools to help youth manage stress, crisis and mental health problems. The goal is to inspire youth to reach out, get help and give help. The website www.mentalhealth4kids.ca has an excellent mental health library with articles about a variety of topics and conditions.

When our daughter was about fourteen she suffered through a period when nothing brought her joy. She confided in me about her unhappiness and we looked for solutions, but my main message was one of empathy and support. "How terrible it must be to feel this way. I am so sorry you're going through this. This will pass and you'll find pleasure in things again." Even in this dark hour, though, she didn't completely lose her sense of humour, as I found out when I gave her a sparkling clear crystal meant to comfort her. "Your outside may get bashed and bruised," I told her, "but the core of your being will always be pure, strong beauty like this crystal." She laughed, and said I sounded like a soap opera. Fortunately, after several weeks, her spirits lifted. I never knew why, I was just enormously relieved. Looking back, she doesn't remember this period, so can't shed any light on what brought her out of the darkness. She's not sure the crystal helped—but it made *me* feel better just to hear her laugh!

Catherine was worried when her son went through quite a lengthy depression. "When my son reached the awkward ages of twelve and thirteen," she remembers, "he seemed confused, unhappy, even depressed. He rarely wanted to talk, and we were at a loss as to how to help him. He wouldn't fall asleep before 2 or 3 A.M. and was always exhausted. He didn't care about his marks and did the absolute minimum of schoolwork. He had trouble making friends and felt excluded at school. But by grade 11 everything had changed. He became engaged in school and his marks improved dramatically. He grew out of the silent period and started to have a wide social circle including more girls. He has become a happy, confident, eloquent young man. I am proud and happy for him, but I cannot say what happened, except that he matured, gained confidence and seemed more focused on how he was being perceived by the world at large, rather than only focusing on his classmates. Through this period we made absolutely sure he knew we cared, and that he could talk to us about anything. We gave him boundaries, but we did not confine him. We let him make mistakes and hoped he would come to us and most of the time he did."

My daughter and Catherine's son were some of the lucky ones. Others, like Simon, had a rougher road to travel. Simon is now in his late twenties and light years away from the torments of his teenage years, but love and support were not enough to bring him out of his pain. In addition to enormous family and social support, he required an intensive treatment program that included hospitalization and appropriate medication, identified through a long process of trial and error. His mother, Linda, says that Simon showed symptoms throughout his early teens, but the really dramatic problems started at about age seventeen. "We confused his early symptoms with typical adolescence," she says, "but now it's easy to see that the problems were much more serious. He became rebellious and distant and shifted his peer groups for the worse. He lost interest in the sports he had always loved, his grades began to suffer, and he was increasingly sad and removed. We began to realize that he was using drugs on a regular basis, and I now understand that he was self-medicating to numb the pain.

"By this time the illness had truly grabbed hold. He became anxious and fearful; he was exhibiting paranoid behaviour and was convinced his family and friends were out to get him; and he began to lose his grip on reality. The physical symptoms were dramatic. He lost a lot of weight, and was gaunt and lethargic. And then began a precipitous decline in which he started to lose all self-respect, including basic concern about clothing and hygiene. We were frantic with worry. 'Tough love' was one of the approaches suggested to us. We tried it, but almost instantly realized that the strategy was completely wrong for Simon. It would have driven him on to the street, and we would never have gotten him back. Throughout Simon's decline we went to a series of doctors, and sought help from the school, and it was really only Simon's football coach/math teacher who understood that Simon was sick. Armed with his advice we travelled hundreds of miles to find mental-health professionals who specialized in treating adolescents. They recognized that Simon had a brain chemical imbalance, and once under their care, he was on the road to recovery."

One of the invaluable resources in Simon's path to wellness was a community support centre for young adults who are living with mental illnesses called Laing House (see p. 263 for the URL) in Halifax, Nova Scotia. The Laing House motto is "Come as You Are." I have used Simon's real name because he and his family have told their story in an education resource package called "The Sooner the Better: Get Help Early for Psychosis," which includes a video and an information guide. The package is available from the Nova Scotia Early Psychosis Program (see p. 263 for the URL).

Based on Simon's experience, Linda says, "If you suspect that your child is in serious difficulty always trust your 'gut instinct,' seek out early intervention and stop at nothing until you find the right resources. Be positive but aggressive, and make sure that all family members and/or friends are on the same page. The last thing your son or daughter needs is a mixed message. Timely action is essential because early diagnosis and treatment is the key to faster recovery."

Helen talks about how rough it was for both her daughter and their family until they finally had her daughter's depression diagnosed. "My eldest daughter went through a rough patch when she turned thirteen," she explains, "and it lasted until she was fifteen. She was eventually clinically diagnosed with seasonal affective disorder (SAD), a form of winter depression that was affecting both her school and family life. I realized something was wrong when I noticed changes that were very worrisome, including anti-social behaviour that was completely out of character for the child we knew. We kept telling her we loved her despite these difficulties; we disciplined her, we fought with her and we were beside ourselves with worry. We kept in mind that no child just goes bad. There are reasons and influences. We devoted our time to getting to the bottom of what was troubling her, and we offered tough love and support. It was a very happy day when the diagnosis was made. Now at nineteen, she tells me of the remorse she feels for being such a difficult child. She tells me far more details of what she went through than she ever revealed when she was younger. I told her that it was not a burden. It's my loving job to be her parent and support her, and I'd do it again a thousand times over because the result was worth it. One lesson this taught me—as a parent you have to be vigilant through the tough early teen years, because you think you are getting the whole truth but you probably are only being told a fraction. Think of all the things your parent didn't have a clue of about you!"

Because they had a suicide in their family, Gloria made a point of educating her son about the signs and symptoms of depression. But all of the stories related above happened to teenagers without known family histories, so Gloria's approach would be a good precaution for all of us. Based on Simon's experience, Linda agrees. "We should make sure that all our children are knowledgeable about brain chemical disorders. And we parents should inform ourselves so that we know how to respond appropriately and take action if needed." Maria reminds us of the importance of medical experts in the diagnostic process. "Our friend's daughter was diagnosed as bipolar and she was medicated and even temporarily institutionalized. After a long painful journey, an MRI [magnetic resonance imaging], ordered by a skeptical psychiatrist, showed a brain tumour that was successfully removed."

Sexual Identity vs. Sexual Confusion

Research has found that teens who identify themselves as gay, lesbian or bisexual, or who are unsure of their sexual identity, are twice as likely as their heterosexual peers to think about or attempt suicide, so it's critical we give them the support they need.[21] Fortunately the online world has made it easier for teens to learn about the many dimensions of sexual orientation. For example, the section "Sexual Attraction and Orientation" on the website www.kidshealth. org is a non-judgemental and thoughtful description of the issue in all its complexity, and emphasizes the importance of finding knowledgeable, empathetic people with whom your teen can talk.[22] The website www.spiderbytes.ca has a section on sexuality that takes a similar approach, with discussion about same-sex attraction, gender identification and tips for coming to terms with your emerging sexuality.

Because it can be hard for LGBT (lesbian/gay/bisexual/transgender) youth to imagine a positive future for themselves, Don Savage set up the *It Gets Better Project* (see p. 263 for the URL). He wanted to show these teens what their lives might be like as openly gay adults and to give them some hope. Savage was motivated by the suicide of a gay teenager in Indiana who killed himself after being taunted by his classmates. Both Savage and his husband were bullied at the Christian schools they attended. He writes, "We are living proof that it gets better. We don't dwell too much on the past. Instead, we talk mostly about all the meaningful things in our lives *now*—our families, our friends (gay *and* straight), the places we've gone and things we've experienced—that we would've missed out on if we'd killed ourselves *then*."[23] When Savage asked people to submit their stories to his YouTube campaign, he received 127 videos in less than a week, and more arrive daily.

Marlene remembers with absolute clarity the day her fourteen-year old daughter told her she might be bisexual. "Tracy had always been happy-go-lucky and well adjusted, and, suddenly she was moody, sad and irritable," Marlene remembers. "I tried to ignore it for a while, thinking it had to do with the usual adolescent stuff, like friends, school, search for self. I was a widow raising three young children, and Tracy was the eldest, so when problems were non-life-threatening I ignored them for the first while. When her mood didn't improve I asked her what was wrong without thinking too deeply about the possibilities. Her tearful response, 'I think I might be bisexual,' left me speechless. I had always prided myself on being an intuitive parent who could predict what might be wrong and offer sage advice or support when needed. But this really taught me a lesson: expect the unexpected when you are dealing with kids. None of my life experiences had prepared me for this kind of revelation, nor for the subsequent conversations that became necessary. I had absolutely no experience with sexual-identity issues and had never imagined this situation.

"Before responding to Tracy, I gathered her in my arms. I was acutely aware that this moment could go either of two ways—good or bad, and whatever I said or did would imprint forever on my daughter's subconscious. I felt this was a pivotal moment in her life, one I felt obligated to make okay with my response. So I started the conversation with something like, 'Tell me why you think this?' It was revealed that she had a crush on a girl in her class at school—a crush with definite sexual overtones.

"My way of dealing with difficult or unfamiliar situations is to gather information through books, professionals, friends and family. So I suggested to Tracy that, with her permission, I would call our pediatrician and ask him to recommend an expert who would know more about this than me, with whom she could explore her feelings. And that's how it started. First a consult and then ongoing meetings with a teen and adolescent pediatrician (who happened to be a lesbian), then support groups with other gay, lesbian and bisexual youth. From there, the process evolved, with my daughter fostering friendships with other similar youth and obtaining information from books and the Internet about being different from most of her peers at school. I didn't vet the resources that she used and trusted the online sources of information as safe. In hindsight, I realize I knew very little about what she was learning from her own sources.

"I could see that Tracy needed to be who she was—which was 'not straight.' Over time the nomenclature for her sexual preference has changed, from 'bisexual' to 'lesbian' to 'queer.' The process of adjustment for Tracy and our family was far from smooth. We didn't share the information with her siblings until Tracy was comfortable with the idea herself. When the time came to disclose to family and close friends, we agreed that it was her story for the telling, not mine. I don't remember how she finally informed her sisters, but I do recall it being a non-issue. But dealing with my friends and family was much more difficult. Tracy's sexual identity would sometimes come out in our response to the question, 'Is Tracy dating anyone?' and we got a variety of reactions. 'She's young—she'll change her mind.' 'Was anyone in your husband's family gay?' 'Oh my God!' Then there were the homophobic remarks—sometimes from people I liked. These comments were hurtful and hard to handle, and I choose to deal with them without involving Tracy. She needed my love, support and complete acceptance about being who she needed to be. Tracy was a leader at her school and she became increasingly confident with her identity. Through her own courage, and with encouragement from me, she became the first one in her all-girl school to attend a school dance with her same-sex date."

Tracy is in her twenties now and completely confident in her sexual identity. I asked Marlene what advice she and

Tracy would have for parents. Marlene replied, "Tracy tells me terrible stories about what has happened in other cases. Some families reject their children, even going so far as to ask them to leave home. Others impose all kinds of rules that force them to deny who they really are in order to conform to their family's ideal. The result can be severe psychological trauma. Tracy met a girl at university who came from a family in which both the parents were university professors. But it can't be assumed that with intelligence and knowledge would come acceptance. Their daughter was boyish in appearance. She had a short, punkish hairstyle and always wore pants. There was nothing feminine about her. When she went home for the holidays her parents would meet her at the airport with a more appropriate outfit for her to change into—a sweater and skirt, along with a wig to wear. She is now estranged from her family and has had an extremely difficult time, including cutting herself and suicide attempts. Tracy tells me, 'I'm so glad you were my parent and that you were non-judgemental.' But I'm not going to minimize the adjustment a parent has to make. I've had to empty my mind of any images I may have had of a picture-perfect family ten to fifteen years in the future."

Marlene urges parents to help their teens develop an emotionally healthy and morally responsible attitude towards sex, regardless of sexual orientation. But she found it more difficult to implement guidelines with a non-straight teen. "I do think that the rules around sexuality that the parents establish for heterosexual teens should be applied equally for teens with other sexual orientations, but I found it harder to establish those same boundaries with my daughter. For example, when boys came to visit my heterosexual daughter, the rule was they could be in her bedroom only if the door remained open. It was harder to enforce that rule with Tracy when I didn't know if the young woman visiting her was a 'special friend' or just a friend. I realize in hindsight that she had more sexual experimentation earlier both because it was easier to hide and because there was no fear of pregnancy."

Education vs. Entertainment

When our teens are watching a TV show or listening to music, we wonder whether they are being entertained or educated, and we know that sometimes it's a bit of both. When my daughter was about eighteen years old she told me about an incident when she had stood up to peer pressure in order to do the right thing. Looking back on our discussion, I don't remember anything about the incident; it's what we talked about afterwards that stuck in my mind. I asked her where she had acquired her strength of character, and who her role models had been. She first credited her sister, then, tactfully, included me, and then named a few other strong women in her life. The final name on her list was Buffy, the Vampire Slayer.

Since I assumed that my daughter (along with her peers) was mainly using television to zone out in front of mindless, dumbed-down entertainment, I was intrigued that she had included a TV character in her short list of role models.

I knew that *Buffy* was her favourite TV program and that DVDs of the show topped her gift wish list, but I hadn't thought much about the life lessons that were being passed along with these hours of fun. As we continued to talk, my daughter gave specific examples of how each of her role models demonstrated strength in their daily lives. She described Buffy as a powerful and good leader who defeats her foes in hard-fought battles of equals. Basically she "kicks ass" over the fate of the world, does so with wit and soul, and looks "hot" while doing so. To my feminist ears this sounded like the unlikely marriage of an action figure with the basics of female empowerment.

Subsequently I discovered there are hundreds of academic papers that analyze the minutiae of Buffy as role model, some of which uphold and some of which dispute her position as a feminist ideal.[24] Regardless of the scholarly debate, you can certainly see the appeal of the character for teenage girls. Buffy's creator, Joss Whedon, said he wanted to create "Barbie with kung-fu grip" and he certainly succeeded. I don't know if other teenage girls and boys have the same emotional response to the show as my daughter, but it was Whedon's hope that they would. "I designed Buffy to be an icon," he says, "to be an emotional experience, to be loved in a way that other shows can't be loved. Because it's about adolescence, which is the most important thing people go through in their development, becoming an adult. And it mythologizes it in such a way, such a romantic way—it basically says, 'Everybody who made it through adolescence is a hero.'" According to my daughter, it's not a bad show for teenagers to watch. Sounds as if it should even be recommended viewing.

This show is an example of the complexity of the issues surrounding popular media and our teens, and the resulting challenges for parents. Was it a good thing that my daughter was allowed to watch this show (actually *encouraged* is a better word if I consider our gifts to her of the show on DVD)? Now that *Buffy* is off the air, are there new shows that offer the same kind of potentially positive role-modelling? My older teen friends tell me that *Twilight*, the vampire-based fantasy series, is useful as a behaviour model, but, in this case, a negative one for unhealthy relationships.

Steven Johnson, author of *Everything Bad Is Good for You*, argues the virtues of TV shows like *Buffy*, not for the content, but because their structural and philosophical complexity trains you to think better. However, even he acknowledges that television can be addictive and time-consuming, and you have to draw the line.

Many of us put viewing restrictions in place for our teens such as: "no TV until your homework is done," "no TV during the school week," "only one show per week—pick the one you want." Over the decade that our children were teens, we tried all these approaches. We even had a period when there was no television in the house. The TV set had broken down and our daughter who was nine years old at the time said, "Let's not get the TV fixed. It's wasting my time." We went without television for months until we adults finally broke down and got the set repaired because we missed watching the news. Eventually TV restrictions became a non-issue because our teenagers were watching so little, or if they were watching it, it was in places where we didn't notice, such as playing DVDs on their computers.

As a result, when we think about controlling TV viewing, we now think of it as a component of the restrictions on our teenager's screen time that we discussed earlier. But Jennifer has raised four children—her youngest is fifteen—and she reminds us that it is a mistake to overlook the content of TV shows. "I have real concerns about what young people are being exposed to in TV programs," she says. "There is a lot of mature content available at all hours and even shows that are written for teens often portray less-than-desirable role models. Networks are not censoring, so parents must restrict our children's viewing, as best we can, and use this as an opportunity for discussion."

When my daughter and her friend were fourteen years old, we caught them with some adult-only movies they had managed to rent from the video store through some deception. I took the two of them out for lunch and in the middle of the meal pointed to a piece of food that had fallen on the floor and asked my daughter to pick it up and eat it. She looked at me in utter horror, assuming I had gone completely mad. "Why won't you do that?" I asked. Her reply was indignant, "Because it would make me sick." I responded, "Yet you would do the same thing to your brain—pick up utter garbage and put it in your head. You think there's a difference, that those images will flow through your mind without sticking, without leaving any impression whatsoever, without doing you any harm. But that's where you're wrong. If what you see is vivid enough and disturbing enough, you may not be able to get it out of your head, and even if you think it's gone, it may come back as nightmares or hallucinations. So treat your brain the way you treat the rest of your body and give it the respect it deserves." I turned to my daughter's friend and asked her what she thought. She was at a loss for words and replied, "We don't talk this way in our house." My daughter rolled her eyes and said, "Lucky you!"

When it comes to music, developments in the digital world are removing some of the family friction, because we're less likely to hear what's being played. Since our teenagers can download their music or swap songs online and then listen to them through earbuds, we may never hear their selections. But we shouldn't underestimate the impact of their listening choices, and many parents are doing their best to keep current with their teenager's musical taste, and establish some guidelines. "I draw the line at misogynous or racist music," Debbie says. "We discuss it, but I won't allow it played in the house, and the kids know why. There is a lot of language that I hate in their music, but some that I tolerate. I let them know that I'm not impressed by it, but I let it go by."

Helen put her foot down when her teenage sons and daughters started buying music with "Parental Advisory" ratings. "I'd begin by saying that I didn't want to hear this in my house," she explains. "But then I'd try to explain the impact of language and try to get it across from their perspective. What if I said to the butcher, 'Yo, what's up. I want some ****ing meat for my sandwich.' And I wouldn't bleep out the swear word. Since this language is worlds away from my normal conversation, the shock value painted a pretty vivid picture of the power of language to change people's impression of you."

A car ride provides one of the few opportunities left to dialogue about music. "When they put their music on really loud in the car," Debbie says, "I could hardly bear it. But there were a few singers I liked, so I made a big deal of liking them. And, knowing I was going to get it loud anyway, I'd request certain groups or singers. I'd tell them how I was so glad that they hadn't been teenagers in the eighties since I couldn't stand acid rock, but *their* music was a different matter. They just loved that I appreciated their music—it was amazingly important to them." I had the same experience as Debbie. My daughters were genuinely delighted when I identified my favourites among their musical selection, and I would receive the related CDs as gifts.

One of the best opportunities for discussion around popular culture was dropped in my lap every morning when I drove my teenage daughters to school and they wanted to listen to a radio station that was hosted by some misogynous "shock jocks." Initially I couldn't bear to listen to these guys, and I was particularly offended by their treatment of a female sidekick (literally and figuratively). I insisted we listen to other stations, but the girls proposed a compromise. We'd listen to the music on the offensive station, since I had to agree that the music was good and, when the hosts started their banter, they would quickly turn down the volume. We began this approach, but soon I realized I was letting a wonderful teaching opportunity slip through my fingers. So I changed horses and insisted that we listen to what the hosts were saying. From then on I talked back to the radio, mocking the offensive puerile chatter and coming up with zinging comebacks. Soon my daughters joined into the spirit of the sport. We all rejoiced when the poor beaten-down sidekick was replaced by another woman who could hold her own and gave as good as she got. She didn't last long. The hosts announced that she had quit, and said, in offended tones, that she had accused them of "being sexist." After that we moved on, the girls graduated, there were no more early-morning car rides, and the station had outlived its usefulness for us.

Practise vs. Preaching

In the online world our teens can choose to spend hours being exposed to values, norms and religious beliefs that are in direct conflict with our way of thinking. The number and range of websites that advocate hate and, sometimes, violence, is staggering, and includes those run by the Ku Klux Klan, supremacists of every ilk, skinheads, anti-gays, anti-immigrants, Holocaust deniers and the lists goes on. Teens can be seduced by the messages on such sites, like the young man my friend knows who became a Nazi follower after spending hours on neo-Nazi websites. But even in less extreme cases, our children are learning life lessons from their online education.

The best counter to these influences is the daily example we set for our teens as we articulate and act on our beliefs. For some parents, organized religion is an important part of this process. But many teens, although they may have participated in faith-based activities when they are younger, drop out when they get older. "Most teenagers don't think going to church on Sundays is *cool*," Maria says, "and mine were no exception. Instead of fighting them head-on over this, I emphasized that attending Sunday service was not the only way to practise their faith. They kept their contact with the church by volunteering in programs for the homeless, and kept in touch with several church leaders who became family friends and visited us at home. It helped that many of their school friends were part of the same community. Two of my four children practise my religion today, and I respect all their choices. My eldest recently thanked me for 'not bugging her about going to church.' We live in a secular, consumer-driven world and a little faith hasn't hurt any of them."

My own interest in attending Sunday church service was sustained well into my teens because of the vibrancy and vitality of the minister, and the relevance of his sermons. Reverend Doctor Goth believed that you must live your faith, not just sermonize about it, and he practised what he preached. His sermons were full of his lived experience—including a story about his marching with Martin Luther King Jr. in Selma, Alabama, that was used to focus attention on black-voter registration. He preached about international issues, about domestic policies, and about day-to-day decision making in the home, and linked them all back to a faith-based philosophy with moral and ethical underpinnings. But what I liked almost as much as listening to him was our family tradition of going to a restaurant after church and debating the issues over our meal. So one way of keeping your teenager connected to your faith is to attend a place of worship with engaging, inspiring and relevant leaders who act on their faith and preach about issues that connect with immediacy to your teenager's world.

One church in our neighbourhood has developed an effective way of hanging on to their teenage congregation by offering a weekly teen drop-in program centred around music, drama and dance. Throughout the year the teens perform for worship services, pageants and other events. The highlight of the year is a musical theatre production complete with live band, multiple costume changes and elaborate sets. The teenagers audition for the lead roles, but there is room for everyone regardless of talent or interest, including jobs in set building, costumes, sound, lighting, makeup and ticket sales. The show has to be performed several nights running in order to accommodate the eager audience, and the productions sometimes tour to other venues. Not only do teenagers want to be part of the program, pre-teens long for the time when they will be old enough to participate. The main challenge with this brilliant solution is the requirement for lots of volunteer-parent hours, ideally from parents with some talent in musical theatre production!

I asked Jennifer, an educator and mother of four, for her advice about keeping our teens connected to faith. She reminds us that we need to be careful not to confuse the practical battles with the theological ones. "Our teenagers' sudden refusals to attend church may have more to do with the fact that they really don't want to get up in the morning than the fact that they are beginning to disagree with a particular dogma," she explains. "Perhaps something as simple as attending a service at a more palatable time could be a solution. It may be that they don't like or trust a particular leader. In this case, the answer may be finding another community that shares the same beliefs. Figuring out the exact nature of the problem would lead to identifying the right approach to solving it."

Jennifer also urges us to maintain an open mind in our discussions with our teenagers, and to show a willingness to dialogue with them and encourage questions. "By ignoring doubt or even simple curiosity, the questioning doesn't go away," she says. "If parents refuse to entertain questions about the family's religion because they want to ensure that their children remain true to their faith, it may only delay their search and perhaps even push them into unnecessary rebellion. Every child needs to make sense of his or her world. In an open relationship, parents share their views for their teenager's consideration. Your teen may not end up sharing the same convictions as you, but there will be mutual respect, and the door will be open for a return to the faith in later life. By demanding acquiescence and absolutes, you may push your teen away, and close the doors of possibility."

This issue has a particular meaning for Jennifer because she converted to Catholicism when she was a university student. She remembers vividly the insightful dialogue she had with her father at the time. "I had just converted and, with all the conviction I could muster, I was saying how important it was to be married in the Catholic church, to raise my children as practising Catholics so that they would raise their children Catholic, because, of course, they would want to be Catholic, etcetera. My father very quietly said, 'What if we had made those demands of you?' I still remember the slow smile that crossed my lips and the 'aha' moment in my mind as I understood his meaning. My parents had raised me in a different faith yet were being very supportive of my choice to convert. At that moment I decided that I would raise my children in the faith of my own choice, but I would be open and accepting of questions, supportive of searches for truth, and in the end, respectful of the choices they would make as adults, young and old."

Things can get complicated further when the parents do not share the same religious beliefs. Jennifer recommends her friend's approach. "My friend wanted to raise her sons in her faith. While her husband was not opposed to it, he did not attend church with her. When the children were young, they accompanied her without complaint. As the boys grew older, they saw that Dad didn't have to go so they questioned why they should be forced. There were challenging times and lots of battles. Over time my friend tired of the battle and continued to attend church, but on her own. However, she had been very careful not to make the boys feel guilty because that would have placed a judgement on their father. As the boys reached adolescence, they took turns accompanying her to church so that she wouldn't have to go alone. Because the door had been left open and they had always been welcome, the boys were free to join her and there was no risk of 'losing face.' They were also saved from being torn between supporting Mom or Dad. My friend was very wise."

If we despair that our teens do not seem to share our faith or participate in our religious practices we would be well-advised to remember the wise words of the philosopher and poet Rumi. "There are hundreds of ways to kneel and kiss the ground."[25] And for some parents, their own religious faith helps them get through the teen years. "Prayer is my number one parenting tool," Teresa says.

The Teen Citizen

Distraction vs. Disrespect

ONE OF THE BEHAVIOURS that adults find both irritating and worrisome is when teens talk on their cellphone or stare at a computer screen while ignoring the people around them. Schools, parents and even teens themselves are attempting to lay down some rules about these matters of cyber-etiquette, but because these technologies are still so new, it's a work in progress. Many families have rules about no calls or texting during meals, and turning cellphones off at night. Sean's family insists he turn the ringer on his cellphone off when he goes to bed, "so the occasional inappropriately late call will not wake me up—or anyone else!"

At Ashley's school cellphones cannot be visible on school property, period. However, she thinks this rule will be renegotiated soon. "This outright ban is starting to irritate everyone—including parents," she says, "Say you've stayed after school for a team practice and you need to call home when you're ready to get picked up, your only option is to use your cellphone. Your phone then gets confiscated by a teacher and put in the principal's office, and then a parent has to go and pick it up. The school is still trying to figure this out, but something has to change."

I asked some teens what rules they have for each other and the question generated a lot of discussion. "There are no rules among our friends, but there should be," Sarah says. "Like, when a person receives a phone call in the company of other people, they should keep the call short and sweet! And now there's a new line to cross. Skype provides another opportunity to cheat. My boyfriend added girls from clubs to his chat list and webcammed with them. He's now my ex-boyfriend."

Although Ginny is only seventeen she has already noticed a deterioration in "netiquette." "Before, there was a certain etiquette about things you should not do on MSN," she says, "such as breaking up with someone. That was something you had to do face to face. Now these standards seem to have disappeared and anything goes. And texting, since you are limited to 160 characters, really limits what you can say—and this leads to a lot of misunderstanding." She worries that people are developing fewer social skills because they allow themselves and each other to hide behind technology. "Kids will text from across the room rather than approaching someone they're interested in. They're afraid of risking a face-to-face rebuff."

We adults can be as guilty of this type of disrespectful behaviour as our teens. We answer our cellphones at mealtimes, text while people are trying to have conversations with us and demonstrate in many ways that the person in front of us does not have our full attention. We shouldn't be surprised when our teens model our behaviour. Barbara used an example of inconsiderate adult behaviour to teach her son some netiquette. "Shortly after my son received his iPhone, we were eating together at a restaurant as a family," she recalls. "My son's phone rang, and he answered it. This became the perfect opportunity to talk about why this should not happen again. I described a dinner I had witnessed where a dad was out with his young son and the dad spent most of the meal on his cellphone. I said, 'Think about the message this gives his son: that talking to someone else is more important than spending time with you.' Meals are an important time to touch base with other family members. We answer no phones when we have dinner. But unless parents bring these issues up, teenagers will not understand the acceptable use of technology."

Since our teens will be living in an ever-changing technological landscape, there will be a constant need to develop new rules of netiquette that will demonstrate courtesy and kindness. We can help them by laying down a foundation that demonstrates respect for one another, and one place to start is with politeness. By using a simple "please" or "thank you" when we talk with them, we are demonstrating more than a societal nicety, we are showing our consideration for one another. As David Elkind, author of *The Hurried Child*, puts it, "When we are polite to children, we show in the most simple and direct way possible that we value them as people and care about their feelings. Thus, politeness is one of the most simple and effective ways of easing stress in children and of helping them to become thoughtful and sensitive people themselves."[1]

And, if you make sure that you model politeness and courtesy in your dealings with your teenager *and* their friends, you have a leg to stand on when you want the same behaviour from them. When my daughter answered one of my friend's friendly questions with a sullen retort, I was able to take her aside later on and point out the difference in my approach. I said, "I am always polite to your friends, and I expect you to extend that same treatment to my friends. I never want to see that kind of rude behaviour again." She got the message.

Respect is something you can't fake. If we talk to our teenager using a skeptical tone of voice or adopt a dismissive body posture, we communicate our lack of respect, regardless of the words we use. As Malcolm Gladwell describes in *Blink*, doctors who used a dominant tone of voice with their patients were more likely to be sued than those who sounded concerned. Medical competency was not the issue. And the researchers didn't need to hear the words the doctors were using. They based their assessment on forty seconds of taped conversation between patient and doctor in which the words were garbled to render them unintelligible, leaving only intonation, pitch and rhythm. Gladwell sums it up as a matter of respect, and says, "the simplest way that respect is communicated is through tone of voice."[2]

Janet recommends dinner-table conversation that is free of technological disruption as a good way for teenagers to practise showing mutual respect. "I am a firm believer in the value of everyone sitting down together as often as possible for family meals. The dinner table is the place where you can discuss and debate issues and clear the air. It's a chance for adults to ask the young people about their points of view and to engage them in dialogue. Once you show them you respect them for their opinions, they'll respect you for yours. And our rule is to always try to leave the table as friends. If someone storms off, try and bring them back and make the necessary apologies."

Debbie emphasizes the importance of respecting teenagers' evaluations of people and situations. "We made it clear to our kids that they had to respect authority, be it at the school, on the hockey rink, on the street or in the local store. However, adults are not always right, and, in fact, they can be bullies, or lazy or 'way off base.' We never held up the adult side as automatically superior, and often commiserated with our kids regarding poor behaviour on the part of adults—a neighbour who worked the socks off them and then was really cheap in paying them, a teacher who was lazy or unfair, or a policeman who abused his authority. I think this kind of communication reinforces the idea that they (the kids) have judgements that are sound and worth respecting. This also provides lots of food for discussion— about looking at things from another person's point of view, about what kinds of behaviour gets people's backs up, about what's fair, etcetera. We were proud of our son last year for getting on well with his summer job boss. The man was known to be difficult, even unreasonable, and we said, 'Unless he's really stepping on your rights, he's the boss and you're the underling, and it's to your advantage to get on with him.' I think part of the reason our son was able to do this was the years of our talking together about people in authority who were less than perfect!"

Helen reminds us that respect also means not talking about "you teenagers" in generalities and lumping all teens together. "Adults hate to be lumped into unhelpful stereotypes as in 'you yuppies,' or 'you men,'" she says. "So do they. And never say, 'What's wrong with you?' Keep the focus on what they are doing that is bothering you, not who they are." And it's useful to remind ourselves of the attitudes teenagers face from the world around them. As Helen found out, "If you want to see how society often treats our young people, go into a store (especially a high-end one), with a teen, walk a few feet behind them, and watch."

But respect needs to be a two-way street. "Don't let your teens get away with insulting you," Janet says. "Some parents seem to tolerate ignorance just to avoid a scene. I say it's far better to make a scene than to condone bad behaviour. Call them on it immediately. We were on a holiday and I was taking a typical tourist photo only to be told by my daughter in a most belittling tone that I had done it all wrong, and the photo was going to be terrible. I said, 'How dare you tell me how I should take a photo! You have no right to talk to me like that.' She walked off in a huff, and then came back and apologized, but in one of those face-saving tones that implied she wasn't really sorry. But the next day she was gracious about our photo-taking, and I was so glad I'd spoken out. It's worth it. Deal with the issue then and there."

Responsibility vs. Entitlement

Today's teens are perceived as having a strong sense of entitlement, to the point where the media has taken to calling them the Me Generation. In his book *Generation Text*, clinical psychologist Michael Osit notes that 83 percent of Americans believe that today's youth have a stronger sense of entitlement than kids did ten years ago. Osit says our child-centred parenting style should take some of the blame, but this failing has been exacerbated by a high-tech world that makes it easier to get things done. The result is a generation that is used to getting what it wants with minimal effort.

According to Osit, problems develop when technology gives our children rewards without requiring hard work; for example, the software that lets them compose their own music without having to put in the hours to learn how to play an instrument. "Technology simultaneously brings kids to new heights of knowledge and information, while negatively impacting the development of the basic work ethic," he writes.[3] Parents exacerbate the problem by letting their teens regularly replace perfectly functioning cellphones, iPods and computers with newer models, simply because the teens want the latest and the best. As a result, he writes, "Working toward potential, or doing your best, is an aspiration that has a dwindling presence among Generation Text kids." He sees lots of kids like Lindsey, a teen with a "good enough" attitude towards her schoolwork. She asks, "Why should I work hard when I am doing okay?"[4] Osit wants parents to examine how we might be contributing to our children's poor work ethic, and urges us to provide our kids with the tools they need to work for what they want.

I read Lindsey's words with a jolt of recognition. When my daughter was in her early teens she told me that she didn't see the point in having to work so hard at school. She said, "I don't want to be rich—so why bother?" I replied, "Unfortunately you don't have a choice—you have an obligation to apply yourself. You have brains, good health and are surrounded by people who love and support you. None of this was earned by you; it was a gift. So it's not about being rich—you have a duty to fulfill your potential and give back to society." Her frustrated response was, "That's not fair." I answered, "Would you have preferred to have been born alone, and without your mental and physical abilities? Think of the unfairness of that." Although she gave a profound sigh, and my logic may have been faulty, I think she found some comfort in the matter-of-factness of my response. There was no ambivalence—burdensome as it was, she had a duty to do her best.

This burden of duty can be a powerful motivating force in the lives of young people. Marian Wright Edelman, founder of the Children's Defense Fund, says that her small-town, segregated childhood in South Carolina was mediated by the voices of parental and community expectation. The message she received was a powerful declaration that "service is the rent we pay for living." She writes: "We were told that the world had a lot of problems; that Black people had an extra lot of problems, but that we were able and obligated to struggle and change them; that being poor was no excuse for not achieving; and that extra intellectual and material gifts brought with them the privilege and responsibility of sharing with others less fortunate."[5]

Thomas Friedman, the best-selling author of *The World Is Flat*, argues that when we let our children think that life is a cakewalk, we're not doing them any favours, and, at the same time, we are jeopardizing the economy. "The sense of entitlement, the sense that because we once dominated global commerce and geopolitics—and Olympic basketball—we always will, the sense that delayed gratification is a punishment worse than a spanking, the sense that our kids have to be swaddled in cotton wool so that nothing bad or disappointing or stressful ever happens to them at school is, quite simply, a growing cancer on American society." He urges parents to make sure their children realize their potential, including encouraging them to work hard and delay some gratification, and helping them see the need to hone their skills. As Friedman notes, other parts of the global economy are hard-working and hungry for self-improvement, so if we don't start to turn things around "our kids are going to be in for a huge and socially disruptive shock from the flat world."[6]

But it takes more than words to convey this message. Our teenagers need responsibilities—whether family duties, community commitments or jobs. Through living these responsibilities on a day-to-day basis, they learn that their contribution is valued and needed, that sometimes they have to consider someone else's needs before their own, and that hard work brings rewards. According to research carried out by the University of Minnesota, whether or not children did chores was the best predictor of their likely success as adults. Lead researcher Marty Rossman thinks this connection between helping out and doing well is the result of young people contributing to something larger than themselves, and that this lays the groundwork for successful integration into the workforce. But Rossman urges parents to establish the pattern well before the teenage years, before their kids are too old to be indoctrinated with the concept "we're all in this together."[7] In my opinion, it's never too late to try, as you'll see from the stories below.

When families run their own businesses, it's not hard to find duties for the teenagers: success depends on everyone sharing the workload. Several years ago Audrey and Trevor built a lodge in a mountain resort area to offer accommodation and fine dining. Their two teenagers are actively involved in the business, participating in everything from developing marketing strategy to waiting on tables and greeting guests. Occasionally the children complain that their parents are giving them chores just for the sake of it, but the reality is that their parents are stretched thin and truly need their help—and the children know it. When

Audrey and her children stayed with her sister's family, she had the chance to compare her children's behaviour with their cousins'. It was then she realized just how much her children have benefited from taking on responsibilities. As she recalls, "The first morning after breakfast was done, everyone got up from the table. My two automatically took their dishes over to the sink and put them in the dishwasher. Their cousins just left their dirty dishes on the table. Vickie, my fifteen-year-old daughter, said to her cousins, 'Are you just going to leave your dishes there?' One of them replied with a grin, 'Don't worry, Mom cleans it up!' Vickie replied, 'Your mom's not your slave!' Vickie later said to me, 'It's shocking how little work they do around the house.'"

It's not just families with the day-to-day pressures of a family business who can find ways to make sure their teenagers take on responsibilities. Victoria says that her children figured out they needed to chip in when they rented a cottage near an "awesome" ski hill. She and her husband were happy cross-country skiing closer to home, but it was the kids who wanted a place where they could downhill ski. "It helped that the children knew we were renting the place for them," Victoria explains, "but what was crucial was letting them pick the cottage. They compared the two options—one had a dishwasher and full bath, and one had a shower only. I would have picked the bath—a consideration they weren't the least bit interested in—but, because they liked the arrangement of the bedrooms better, they picked the one without the dishwasher. Making the decision also made them take on the responsibilities involved—

dishwashing by hand. Also, renting a place, rather than buying, turned out to be the best motivator to get the kids to pitch in. Because we had to renew our commitment every year, they understood that the chores had to get done or we wouldn't be happy, and we wouldn't want to come back."

Eleanor says that teenagers need to pitch in with cooking and cleaning. "When my son and daughter turned thirteen they started making meals," she says, "and they (and their dad) were in charge of one sit-down family supper a week. They could share or divvy it up, but the food had to be on the table when Mom came home at 7 P.M. from choir practice. No hamburgers, no hot dogs, no pizza, no steak and salad, and no repeats. It meant that a recipe had to be read, the shopping had to be done and the timing had to be figured out. All without consulting Mom, because she was out of the house. Now the kids are known by their friends to be amazing cooks. It makes them beam with pride, and makes me sigh with relief. When Ron was about fifteen, he came home after a sleepover and exclaimed that all the parents everywhere liked him *so* much, and he had decided the reason was that he always helped with the dishes after meals. Then he thanked me for making them do them at home for all these years, because he really liked being liked."

When it comes to keeping their own rooms tidy, however, many of us think teenagers should be given a break. Throughout the teenage years, I referred to our daughters' top-floor dormer rooms as being in the style of "Anne of Green Gables on acid." To the casual observer they seemed truly chaotic, but my daughters claimed they knew where everything was. (That is, except when they couldn't find it.) Since the rooms were infrequently tidied, we tried to enforce a rule of "no food storage" to reduce the chances of vermin infesting the place. But aside from the removal of dirty dishes, there was limited interference in either their "design choices" or neatness standards. I firmly believe that teenagers' rooms should be their sanctuary. This is one thing that you can safely leave in their hands at a time when most other things are out of their control.

But the best way to learn about duty and responsibility is through good work experiences. Both of our daughters worked every summer from the age of fourteen, and one of them also worked part-time during the school year. The research findings on teenagers and work are pretty consistent. High-school seniors who work up to twenty hours per week tend to perform better academically than those who don't. But twenty hours seems to be the healthy upper limit, with adolescents who work more reporting higher levels of emotional distress. On the plus side, positive work experiences can be associated with increased leadership skills and career motivation. On the down side, students who work are more likely to smoke and drink than non-working students.[8]

Marilyn first encouraged her daughter to get a job as a way of teaching her about the value of money, and found there were additional payoffs. "I was prepared to buy her winter boots, but not expensive designer boots, so she had to make up the difference. To help her out, I encouraged her to pursue her Royal Lifesaving designation and swimming instructor qualification so that she would have the necessary credentials to apply for well-paid summer jobs and part-time positions. She will be wonderful in that role, and has been offered a part-time job teaching at her swim club next school year. I also encouraged her to take a babysitting course, and she has made good money that way. And truly, she enjoys being in charge and doing a job. In many ways it brings out the best in her. Not incidentally, it provides her with much more discretionary cash. Spending money she has earned herself is far better thing than spending the parental dole."

But it matters what kind of work your teen is doing. Not every job has redeeming value, and the gains from working may be offset by an exploitative company, a depressing atmosphere or an unsafe worksite. In contrast, our daughters worked in arts organizations where they were given responsibility, had opportunities to grow and to learn, and were exposed to admirable role models. They learned countless lessons—the value of money when you've earned it yourself, the importance of a good working environment and the satisfaction of a job well done. They also got the kind of experience and references that looked good on their résumés.

Financial Acumen vs. Spending Skills

Given that money, or rather the lack of it, is one of a teenager's main concerns[9], it is unfortunate that this is the subject many parents feel most uncomfortable discussing. Money looms even larger than sex, drugs and alcohol as a topic we want to avoid. A teen's money worries may be immediate, such as not having enough money for a coffee, or long term, such as not being able to afford a university education. And when their opinion is asked, they say they consider their parents their most trusted source for information on finances, and that they want our help.[10] We should be seizing the opportunity to teach our teens practical skills such as budgeting, provide ways for them to learn money management first hand, and talk honestly and openly to them about our finances.

The digital world puts some new financial strains on teen and family budgets, which offer perfect opportunities for talking money with our children. Cellphone plans need to be negotiated with our teen, and agreements made around limitations on text and voice usage. According to a Pew Survey one in three teen cellphone users are on a family plan with limited voice minutes and one in four are on a family plan with unlimited minutes. Three-quarters have unlimited texting. Not surprisingly, teens' use of cellphones is strongly associated with the type of plan they have and who pays the phone bills, with those on unlimited plans where someone else pays talking and texting the most.[11]

Then there's the challenge of online purchases. Downloads, whether a song, an app or a game component, often require a credit card, and then there is eBay and all the other alluring online stores. Some banks offer prepaid credit cards to teens as young as thirteen, which allows them to upload money and spend until they reach the limit, with no line of credit extended. A credit officer says these prepaid cards are useful for older teens as long as the parents aren't the ones loading the cash onto the card and paying the fees themselves. "The children aren't learning as much," she says, "as they would if [they were] uploading the credit card, checking balances and understanding that every time they do all this, they're losing money."[12] Marilyn describes her relentless efforts to teach her teenage daughter the value of money, and the important life skill of living within one's means. "Money has been an ongoing bone of contention between Ella and me," she says. "It is really about the *value* of money and the sense of entitlement. Ella has a large concept of what she deserves in life. Almost reflexively, if anyone ever got anything, she felt intensely aggrieved if she did not get the same thing or an equivalent. These days teenagers seem to expect and get a lot, from unlimited cellphone use to designer coffees to evenings at clubs. As a parent in charge of running a household, I am always looking for ways to spend less. That is my focus. It is the opposite with Ella, who delights in finding ways to spend, the more the better. So we have many head-knockers. I tell her that as a parent I am responsible to feed and clothe her, house and educate her. I tell her that I will support her learning skills and arts, sports and camp. But anything else is gravy. Her allowance is partly discretionary—spending money for whatever she wants—but primarily it is to provide her with the money she needs for things that I would pay for if I were there, such as bus tickets. If she wants to dye her hair, that is her affair, and she must pay for it. She may choose what to spend her discretionary allowance on, but she has to live with her choices. I've become pretty hard-nosed about this, because I want her to understand that her parents are not an endlessly exploitable source. If she overuses her cellphone, for which I pay the basic plan, then she has to pay me back, or I dock her next allowance. I explain that only she can control her use of her phone, so the consequences of overuse must be hers. As for her clothing allowance, it could not possibly be big enough for her desires, but I do not bail her out if she splurges on some things and forgets she needs new jeans. I do endure a lot of cogent arguments about whether the amounts are fair and, sometimes, Ella wins.

"The point is," Marilyn says, "when you have a teenager who desires so much stuff and is a little impulsive, it is important to teach her that once money is spent, it's gone. It takes amazing stamina to hold to that principle! I am fuelled also, to be honest, by a visceral kind of reaction to that careless sense of entitlement that Ella and many of her friends seem to have. It offends me and I tell her so. So time will tell if this value confrontation will work. It's been two or three years of arguing, but, touch wood, I feel as if we have achieved some acceptance of the operating principle. Ella has even been heard to remark on the careless spending habits of her friends!"

Opportunities to acquire and practise financial skills can come from many sources, including participating in household budgeting. My friend who was a single mom paid her two teenage sons to be her accountants. They kept track of her entire portfolio on a spreadsheet, and they knew her complete financial picture. This level of involvement may be too much for most of us, but it really paid off in her case. Because her boys knew exactly what her pocketbook could tolerate, negotiations about money were made easier. When she was killed in an accident before her sons were out of their teens, her decision to develop their financial skills and provide them with full disclosure turned out to be a godsend.

A perfect chance to improve my daughter's budgeting skills arose when she and her two friends were looking for an apartment to live in when they started university. The mother of one of the friends called me in a panic to say that the three girls had their hearts set on a place that was going to bankrupt us all, and she didn't want to be the one to say "no." I knew it would be best if the girls came to this decision on their own, so I agreed to meet with them and the prospective landlord. After the meeting, I asked the girls to draw up a simple spreadsheet comparing the apartment's rent and their other living expenses to their budget. However, before they calculated the bottom line, I insisted we sit down and have a good meal together. I have learned the hard way that negotiations should not be conducted on an empty stomach, especially if that stomach belongs to a teenager. After lunch the three of them wanted me to look at their data sheet and make the decision. But I handed the sheet back to them, and asked them to draw their own conclusion. Looking at the numbers, they faced the obvious— they couldn't afford the place of their dreams. Rather than being the bearer of bad news, I was left in the much more comfortable position of being the one to commiserate with them.

My father bought all three of his children a nominal number of shares in blue-chip companies when we were young and taught us the basics of the stock market. As for our children, we concentrated on helping them learn about personal banking, budgeting and responsible credit card use. Having jobs and earning their own money from the age of fourteen made them increasingly careful consumers. But it was the experience of a friend of mine that made me realize we had to be really up front with our children about their financial future. Over lunch one day Ellen told me with some bitterness that she had just found out that she was not going to get an inheritance from her family. At this point she was in her forties, and had made career choices based on the assumption that she would be receiving a substantial amount of money from her parents. Looking back, she realized she had been operating on unspoken and incorrect assumptions. As it stood, she would likely never be able to afford the kind of lifestyle she wanted and she felt angry and betrayed.

Based on Ellen's experience, I realized we had to lay out our children's future financial prospects for them in black and white, before they made career choices based on any false assumptions. We had one such discussion when my daughter was fifteen. Over lunch one day, we told her the full extent of our financial commitment to her—we would help support her while she completed her post-secondary education, and we would do our best not to be dependent on her in our old age. She looked taken aback when the message sunk in—that once she'd completed her education she would be on her own financially. However, she quickly adapted. Later that day she phoned me from her cousin's house. She and her cousin had fallen in love with New York City from watching many episodes of *Friends*, and their long-range dream of the moment was to launch their careers in the Big Apple. The reason for her phone call was to tell me that she'd figured out how to keep their plan intact even with the knowledge that she would be financially on her own. She wanted to know whether we would be willing, when the time came, to kick-start her future by covering the costs of her monthly subway pass. She figured she could make a go of it in NYC as long as she could afford to get around to the cheapest stores. We learned from this experience that teenagers adjust very rapidly to new realities. We just need to keep them informed.

But if we really don't want to tackle the money subject alone, help is available from a number of excellent resources, and, in the process of researching, we might learn something ourselves. The Canadian Bankers Association website (see p. 264 for the URL) includes resources for students covering a wide range of topics—from the big picture of economic indicators and interest rates, to personal budgeting tips and the basics of credit. There are lots of worthwhile activities, including a personal profiler that guides you through a series of questions to help you get a handle on your spending habits, priorities, strengths and downfalls, as well as a chart that lets you compare the features, fees and interest rates on the credit cards you're considering to figure out which is the best one for you. The section on planning for your future gives advice on achieving educational goals, entering the workforce and assessing whether you have what it takes to be an entrepreneur.

The Investor Education Fund website (see p. 264 for the URL) has interactive modules for students with tips on tracking spending, building wealth and the implications of buying on credit. There are games to play and multimedia tools including worksheets for budgeting and goal setting, as well as a cash-flow spreadsheet. Another useful website is provided by Junior Achievement, the international non-profit organization that educates young people about business and economics. The website (see p. 264 for the URL) includes a JA Student Center, which offers tips to help students become workforce-ready, gain knowledge on handling money, explore careers and start a business of their own.

Good advice and practical tips for raising financially responsible teenagers can be found in Neale Godfrey's book *Money Still Doesn't Grow on Trees: A Parent's Guide to Raising Financially Responsible Teenagers and Young Adults*. Godfrey is a former banker and a mother of two. Her book covers the basic financial facts, including savings and chequing accounts, credit and debit cards, taxes and investments. Equally important is the emphasis Godfrey places on taking a good look at ourselves to understand where our children get their attitudes towards money, and she includes real-life stories of families coping with money issues. There are step-by-step worksheets for you and your teen, and fun quizzes.

What's Right vs. What's Wrong

The digital world facilitates new modes of business transactions and new ways of conducting our affairs that can muddy the line between right and wrong for our teens (and ourselves). Let's take copyright as an example. The Internet allows us to steal the work of artists with ease, and copyright theft is becoming the norm, rather than the exception. Peer-to-peer file swapping of movies and music currently accounts for up to 80 percent of Internet traffic, and during these transactions no artists, creators or producers are compensated. The fear is that we are raising a generation that will expect to have free access to all media. And this is not just a problem with our kids. A vice-president in charge of new media at the performing-rights organization BMI sums up the problem. "People do believe in copyright. But . . . they don't want to pay." Businesses that use the products of artists often don't see themselves in the equation, even when they understand the right of artists to get paid for their work.[13] But whether or not users want to pay, respecting copyright is the right thing to do, and it is also the law. Just so you know, BMI has not lost a single case that has gone to court.[14]

"Illegal downloading is very tempting for teens," admits Barbara, "especially when the whole world seems to be doing it, including their parents. In the days of Napster,[15] we eagerly embraced the idea of file sharing and continued with our use of programs such as Limewire.[16] It took us a while to do the right thing, but now we do, and we've been clear with our son about not illegally downloading music and movies. We have explained the legal ramifications, as well as the right of artists to earn income from their work. It's a tough battle, particularly when teens need to live within a budget, which means they can't purchase as much music as they would like. This makes illegal downloading all the more tempting, but it's important to stand firm. I have my son's word that he is following the rules, but I will not go as far as checking his computer. I trust him and would not want him to think otherwise."

What can add to the dilemma for teens (and for all of us) is the reality that the fine line between theft and downloading shifts daily, and the right thing to do is not always obvious in every case. Creative Commons is a non-profit organization founded in 2001 with the purpose of creating a more flexible copyright model, replacing "all rights reserved" with "some rights reserved." These licences allow creators to decide which rights they reserve and which ones they waive in order to allow others to share and build upon their work, legally. Then there's open-source software, which prides itself on being free. Open-source developers let people copy, share, change and redistribute their software as long as they do the same with whatever software they develop. Wikipedia is a good example of an open-source model, with contributors making unpaid contributions to an online encyclopedia that is available, free. In

The Pirate's Dilemma, Matt Mason talks about these developments and argues that youth culture is reinventing capitalism. He lauds Creative Commons for permitting a remix of ideas, which will unleash creativity in new ways. "The remix is a legitimate way to create new art, culture, products and ideas from old ones," he writes. "The only thing that's left to remix is our outdated copyright laws."[17] He says that today's pirate is tomorrow's pioneer, but what isn't clear is the economic model that will permit this transition.

As parents we need to be sensitive to the changing landscape, yet stand firm on the rights of creators to be compensated and the need to follow the law. The stance we take on these issues establishes standards of behaviour for our teens to follow. I saw this when my daughters gave their father a set of music CDs for his birthday one year. They had spent hour upon hour searching for just the right road music, and had compiled dozens and dozens of songs from across the decades that would get him groovin' in his car. Their dad was touched deeply by the gift and by the effort they had taken to personalize the collection to his taste. And when they presented the CDs they had one final gift to announce. "Dad, we paid to download every song," they said proudly, knowing the importance he places on respecting copyright.

Then there is plagiarism, another unethical practice that the online world has turned into child's play. As with copyright theft, the issues are not always obvious, and our teens need to be taught research and writing skills that spell out the difference between referencing and plagiarizing.

Joan says that her daughter learned this lesson the hard way. "While writing a paper for her final exam, Megan did her research using a cut-and-paste method and then reworked things into her own words," she explains. "Whether through laziness, rushing or forgetfulness, she left one piece exactly as she had taken it from the Internet. As per the school board's policy of zero tolerance for plagiarism, she received no marks at all for that part of the exam. Lesson learned."

Attitudes towards copyright theft and plagiarism are just some of the many values we are transmitting to our children every day, whether consciously or not. Helping them become adults with a sense of integrity and moral purpose is good for them, as well as being in our own best interest, because their future behaviour as citizens and leaders will affect us all. The American developmental psychologist Howard Gardner argues that the "ethical mind" is one of the "five minds" that will be critical for the future because "as workers and as citizens, we need to be able to act ethically—to think beyond our own self-interest and to do what is right under the circumstances."[18]

There are daily tests in which we are challenged to model ethical behaviour for our children, and you'll find the following example a familiar one. My husband and I and our two daughters had pulled into a parking space in a shopping mall. Our daughter threw the door open and hit the next car—a freshly painted custom car that was obviously lovingly maintained by its owner. We got out and looked at the other vehicle's car door and, sure enough, there was a mark that rubbing couldn't remove. The damage wasn't serious, but it was noticeable—especially on such a well-tended vehicle. We looked around and no one had witnessed the event. So we had the obvious option, but we took the one we would have appreciated if the shoe had been on the other foot. We left a card under the windshield wiper that gave our contact details, explained what had happened and said we would like the owner to call and discuss the situation. We knew that our teenagers were watching and learning. Interestingly enough, we never heard from the car owner.

Maria tells a story about the time she insisted on knowing the truth in order to deliver a message to her daughter about the importance of honesty. "Sandra was about fourteen or fifteen when she and a friend helped themselves to a bottle of homemade wine while they watched a movie at home. My husband and I had gone out for the evening. When we came home it was obvious to us that Sandra was drunk, but she swore she hadn't had a drop to drink. The empty bottle was stuffed between the cushions on the sofa, and even when faced with the cold, hard evidence she still denied everything. Her friend admitted the truth, and added that she hadn't liked the wine. So I concluded that Sandra had pretty much drunk the whole bottle. It took about five days before she admitted the truth. She knew how upset I was, and I kept telling her that I would have more respect for a person who did wrong and owned up to it than for a person who lied. I so wanted her to tell me the truth that I then hit her with the silent treatment. I didn't care about the wine, it was the lying that bothered me. Finally, I sat down and I told her I wouldn't rest until she came clean. She finally relented, told me the truth, and all was well again between us. I told her that whatever she does, even if it's something she's less than proud of, never to be afraid to tell us. Trust is broken with repeated lies. Years later Sandra told me that she had learned a lesson from the wine-bottle battle."

Intervening vs. Standing By

When it comes to bullying and sexual harassment there are no fine lines, and the adult world needs to intervene. It is probable that your teenager will experience bullying or sexual harassment, whether as victim, perpetrator or witness. More than one-quarter of teens say they are sometimes bullied to a point that makes them feel very sad, angry or upset.[19] These behaviours can leave lifelong scars on both victims and aggressors. Increasingly the adult world is realizing that "girls will be girls" or "boys will be boys" is not an adequate response to the problem. And our teenagers need to know that by witnessing bullying and remaining silent, they become perpetrators themselves.

By increasing the speed with which bullies can spread their message and vastly expanding the size of the net they can cast, the online world has taken bullying to a whole new level. The website www.cyberbullying.org explains the forms that cyberbullying can take, from incidents in chatrooms to e-mail content to instant messaging, and discusses ways to track down the perpetrators. The site has good tips for your teen, including never responding to cyberbullies and never giving out secret passwords or PIN numbers, even to friends. Teens need to know that people can use this information to impersonate them and send hateful messages under their name, as in Stephanie's situation, described earlier in the book. If your teen is the recipient of a hateful message about himself or someone else, the recommended approach is to Stop, Block and Tell. He needs to stop what he is doing, block that person immediately and tell a trusted adult. This strategy will prevent him from replying and possibly becoming a cyberbully himself.

When Joan's daughter was bullied, she handled the situation in a way that made Joan proud. "Another student attempted to set Megan's hair on fire. Megan reported the incident to the school authorities, the police were called in and the girl was charged with assault. As a result, my daughter was threatened by the other girl's friends (with comments such as "snitches get stitches") and a hate group against my daughter was set up on Facebook. When my daughter was told about the site she promptly reported it to Facebook, who shut it down. I feel she handled both the incident and the follow-up in a mature and proper way."

While Joan acknowledges that the online world gives a wide audience to those who want to denigrate others, she finds that teenagers are developing their own ways of dealing with cyberbullying. "They are very quick to come to the support of a friend who is being 'dissed' on Facebook or wherever," she says. "Megan has learned to delete friends who are mean or hurtful, to block on her phone the numbers of people who are calling for nasty reasons and to delete unopened e-mails or texts from someone who is not a friend. And, when she got a new phone, she took the opportunity to get a new number, so that unwanted former friends could no longer contact her."

Catherine feels that the bullying her son and daughter endured in their early teens altered them forever. She says, "In some ways, the change was for the better, because they grew into more aware people, but, nonetheless, they have been scarred for life." In the case of her son, she and her husband made the decision not to interfere, a decision she now regrets. "My son was bullied by smaller boys who made jokes about his appearance, his personality, his clothing. He didn't know how to handle the bullying, and he became very depressed. The school, while not condoning bullying, did very little about it, and preferred to see it as 'boys will be boys.' It came to blows one day. Fortunately, my son, who was much bigger, was able to frighten the other boys, and didn't hurt them. He gained confidence from this, and they left him alone after that. But he has never been confident of his friendships and, to some extent, it's because of the bullying. Many of his best friends are girls, which is not a bad thing—but a little sad. And I think somewhere inside he still believes that those bullies might have been right— that he is the 'loser' they made him out to be."

During the period her son was being bullied, Catherine tried several confidence boosters for him that she would recommend to others. "I realized my son was not nearly as quick with the retorts as the boys who were picking on him. So I bought him a copy of the book *1001 Insults, Put-Downs, and Comebacks*, which proved to be such a valued resource for him he that he even took it to camp. I also enrolled him and a friend in improvisation sessions for young people, delivered by actors, to help him develop his verbal skills."

When Catherine's daughter was bullied, she decided to intervene. "My daughter was bullied by the three girls who were supposed to be her 'best friends.' They taunted her and excluded her from things. I believe it was rivalry and envy. After my son's experience, I wanted to handle it differently, but I was nervous about making the situation worse. I went to the school principal and vice-principal, and they spoke to the girls, and then they talked to their parents. As a result, the girls felt very sorry for what they had done. It seems they were young enough not to realize how deeply they were hurting my daughter. My daughter was very shaken by this experience. She had known these girls since nursery school and never really forgave them. She continued to talk to them, but the friendship was never the same. It made her stronger, but it altered her sense of what a friend is and whom she can trust. Now she seems to know who can potentially be a bully and stays clear of them."

Sometimes the bullying can take the form of a long-standing relationship. "Carly reached in at grade seven and grabbed hold of my daughter Virginia," says Helen, "and only let go in second-year university. I was originally thrilled that my daughter had a 'best friend,' but gradually I began to see that the relationship was all about Carly. Virginia was only interested in Carly, and Carly treated her like dirt. Carly insisted on her agenda, wanted her way on the clothes standard, and made it impossible for Virginia to have any other friends. I asked for help from the guidance teachers at school, and from my friends who had girls, and we all came up short. I still don't know what I would have done differently. In the later teens, Carly used my house as her own, had her boyfriends over when I was not at home, and they damaged and stole things. I now see that I was an enabler, and I was somehow trying to project my own idealized image of 'best friend' onto this relationship. I had not given my daughter any tools to deal with bullies. I am eternally grateful that no danger came to either girl in this period (that I know about anyway). It is painful for me to write about this."

The Bully, the Bullied, and the Bystander by Barbara Coloroso includes a chapter on cyberbullying and is an excellent resource for parents. Coloroso includes a list of behaviours that differentiate teasing from taunting, flirting from sexual bullying, and reminds us that bullying is about contempt, "a powerful feeling of dislike toward somebody considered [by the bully to be] worthless, inferior, and undeserving of respect."[20] She has a chapter each on what to do if you have a bully, a target of a bully, or a not-so-innocent bystander in your home. Included in the book is a section on how to help your teen become the antithesis of a bully, i.e., a witness, resister, and defender.

In *Bullies, Targets, and Witnesses: Helping Children Break the Pain Chain*, SuEllen and Paula Fried sum up the skills we need to give our young people in the acronym SCRAPES: social skills and self-esteem, conflict resolution and character education, respect for differences, assertiveness and anger management, power and problem solving, empathy and sexuality. In a section on strategies for students, the authors include suggestions for both the bully and the victim, coupled with case studies. One of the victim strategies proposed by a thirteen-year-old boy is *Cool Down* (don't react), *Confuse* (respond with a random sentence), *Comeback* (learn to think on your feet), and *serve as Consultant* (advise the bully he has to give up the idea of always being in control).

Rachel Simmons' book *Odd Girl Out: The Hidden Culture of Aggression in Girls* includes a chapter for parents and teachers on actively intervening to create environments that do not tolerate meanness. She gives parents examples of what not to say ("it's a phase" or "it happens to everyone, honey") and suggests alternatives including, "Oh, honey. That is so terrible. I'm sorry." And you should add, if you can, "It happened to me." Simmons feels that our best hopes for changing the hidden culture of girls' aggression are teachers, and she offers specific strategies for the classroom. But she urges you to obtain permission from your child before approaching the school. She also warns that you can over-empathize. If you feel his or her pain too deeply and end up weeping and wailing, your teen may decide that it's too stressful to discuss these things with you.

Jennifer, who has seen the issue from both the perspective of parent and teacher, agrees that parents can make the mistake of "over-discussing" the problem, inadvertently blowing things out of proportion and exacerbating things. Joan is sensitive to this issue because her daughter was starting to over-identify as the victim. "Megan is quite sensitive," Joan explains, "and when she was teased at school, she generally responded with tears, which, of course, prompted further teasing and resulted in her feeling that she was always being bullied. As an only child, she didn't grow up with the experience of sibling teasing and rivalry and, because we were older parents few of our friends had children of her age. I have tried to teach her how to react to teasing, including walking away. While I agree with zero tolerance for bullying, as children become teenagers they need to realize that not everyone in the world is going to be nice to them, and sometimes they have to live with unpleasantness and learn to put it behind them otherwise they'll become a perpetual victim."

Over the years Megan has used creative expression to address her concerns about bullying. "She has written a series of poems," Joan says, "both about people who succumb to bullying and who rise above it. Several of her poems were chosen for display in her school's guidance office. She has done a photographic essay on bullying of gay youth and expressed herself through song lyrics." The website www.bullying.org provides a space for young people to tell their stories, whether they have been victim or bully. The message of the site is "Where you are not alone," and contributors submit drawings, multimedia, poems, stories and music. A filter allows you to view the submissions by age, whether child, teenager or adult. Another useful website, www.stopbullyingnow.hrsa.gov/kids/, is designed by and for kids and teens and uses animated characters to portray bullying situations and show appropriate responses. There are resources for adults on what they can do.

Dr. Jill Murray wrote the book *But I Love Him* to help us protect our teenage daughters from controlling or abusive dating relationships. Murray worked as a therapist at a shelter for battered women and children and found that virtually all of the women there began their abusive relationships in high school. Although the women ran the gamut of class, race and education, they shared certain patterns of behaviour, including the fact that they found their partner's possessiveness and attempts at control very flattering—at first. Murray's book includes a chapter on how to prevent abuse. She itemizes the differences between a relationship based on power and control versus one based on equality, and urges us to look at our own family dynamics and role-modelling. She includes tips on how to recognize the warning signs of abuse, a checklist to help spot a potential abuser, and recommends medical, legal and psychological interventions. Murray also has a chapter about girls who abuse boys. She points out that this abuse often goes unreported and advises parents of abusive daughters on how to tackle the problem.

A woman whose nineteen-year-old daughter was murdered by a former boyfriend established the website www. speerssociety.org to address youth relationship abuse. The website describes the warning signs, gives tips for supporting victims and helping abusers and has a section on the particular problems teens face when they're dealing with abuse. These problems include peer pressure, lack of control, safety concerns, poor information, low self-esteem and lack of community support. The site includes a number of scenarios developed in association with the Ontario Psychology Association that set out a variety of abusive situations and give advice on how to help. Another site to explore is www.safeyouth.gov run by the National Youth Violence Prevention Resource Center. Their motto is "stop youth violence before it starts" and resources include fact sheets on bullying and teen dating violence.

The goal of the website www.EqualityRules.ca is to encourage equal, healthy relationships between boys and girls, and there are separate sections for kids and teens. The site uses a school-like setting including three main areas to explore: the locker, the bulletin board and the counsellor's office. Click-on scenarios show boys insulting, controlling or ridiculing girls, including a case of harassment through text messaging. The site's objective is for girls to recognize abuse and learn how to counter it, and the scenarios include suggestions for the girls on how to respond. An equally important goal is to model appropriate behaviour for boys, and the boys in the scenarios demonstrate how to behave. There are lists of tips both for boys and girls, quizzes and links to additional information.

Global vs. Insular

When our teens are roaming the World Wide Web, we hope they are using cyberspace to expand their horizons and rethink their assumptions, rather then being drawn to experiences that reinforce their stereotypes. As future citizens and employees, teens with good international, inter-cultural and inter-gender skills will have an edge, and, if they know where to look, the online world can help them acquire these skills.

Your teen could be learning about dispensing food aid in the United Nations game *Food Force* (see p. 264 for the URL), or applying techniques of non-violent strategy in *People Power* (the URL is also on p. 264), a game based on historically inspired conflicts against dictators, occupiers, colonizers and corrupt regimes. The online game *Darfur Is Dying* (the URL is also on p. 264) teaches young people about the genocide in the Sudan, with the hope that increased awareness will encourage them to take action. The player assumes the role of a displaced person who must manoeuvre against deadly forces in order to protect his refugee camp. The game was developed with input from humanitarian workers on the ground in Darfur.

In *Peacemaker* (see p. 264 for the URL), the player assumes either the role of the Israeli prime minister or the Palestinian president. The player must establish a stable resolution to the Middle East conflict before her term in office ends by reacting to events ranging from military attacks to diplomatic negotiations and by interacting with other political leaders and social groups. The game designers hope the player will learn that peace and cohabitation are worth struggling for, and gain a better appreciation of the complexity of the issues.

Ayiti (see p. 264 for the URL) is an online game developed by high-school students that asks you to help a poverty-stricken family in Haiti to make ends meet and get ahead. The player helps the parents and their three children make decisions about work, education, community building, personal purchases and health care, with the goal of improving their future. The purpose of the game is to show, both realistically and sensitively, the challenges posed by poverty in daily life (specifically in the context of the global right to an education).

Spending time with people from other countries and being exposed to other cultures offers teenagers tremendous opportunities for personal growth. When I was a teenager we lived in a pretty culturally homogeneous town, but what changed the complexion for me was my father's membership in the service club Rotary International. Thanks to Rotary Exchanges, we had visitors from around the world, including India, Japan and Australia, who stayed with us anywhere from several weeks to several months. When my world at the time felt very small and the events of my life seemed dull and uninteresting, these visitors opened windows onto a whole big world just waiting out there. After their visits, my family maintained contact with the guests for a while, but eventually the letters petered out and the connections were lost. These days, if your teen makes international friendships, the Internet allows them to be maintained easily. At the time of writing, 70 percent of Facebook's users are outside the United States and the site operates in more than eighty languages.[21]

Rotary is still encouraging these global connections and, through Rotary Youth Exchange, local clubs sponsor thousands of young people every year in international exchanges lasting from a few weeks to a full academic year.[22] The website Transitions Abroad (see p. 264 for the URL) is a good overview site for information about high-school study abroad, including high-school exchanges and gap years overseas. Also, check out your local YM/YWCA. "Word of mouth is the best way to go on this," Helen recommends. "Every parent you ask has some experience or knows someone who has done this. Ask around."

Developmental psychologist Howard Gardner agrees with the importance of helping our teens understand people who are different from ourselves. In his book *Five Minds for the Future*, Gardner argues that a respectful mind is a requirement for future success and urges us to participate in programs that bring about better understanding and increase mutual respect across cultures. "The world of today and tomorrow is becoming increasingly diverse," he writes, "and there is no way to cordon oneself off from the diversity. Accordingly, we must respect those who differ from us as well as those with whom we have similarities."[23]

Helen has made opportunities for international travel for her daughter a priority, even on the salary of a single mom. "She always comes back from her trips older and wiser, and in a better frame of mind than when she left." Helen says. "If it's a priority, you can always find the money. The payoff is enormous, and it doesn't need to be expensive. There are lots of programs out there that won't break the bank, including high-school exchanges and groups like Children's International Summer Villages (CISV).[24] When my daughter was eleven years old, some families in our community used CISV to organize an exchange with Argentina. A dozen of their young people visited us for one month, and then ours went to Argentina for the same period. It was great. Then, in her late teens, my daughter went to language school in Costa Rica and lived with a local family. This experience was the best of all, and worth every penny in terms of the coping skills she acquired. A few years later she did the same thing in Spain. Every time she went away she came back years older in experience."

Eleanor feels that travelling in Third World countries was probably the single best thing they have done as a family. "Going without the normal comforts of home leads everyone to respect each other's discomfort and lend support," she says. "When we cared about others, we became closer." Eleanor feels the travel has had a positive impact on her daughter's character. "When we went to Ethiopia she concluded that the only thing that separated her from the Ethiopians she met was the incredible luck of her birth place. She remains a thoughtful, caring, thankful young lady, ready to travel and give back. Time will tell, but I think she will do great things. She is compassionate, devoted and ready to be different from the crowd."

The Teen Body

Self-Acceptance vs. Self-Aversion

OCIAL MEDIA SITES, with their harsh personal judgements, and reality TV shows, with their critical peer assessments, can add to the enormous pressure our teens feel to conform to an ideal body type. In *Branded: The Buying and Selling of Teenagers*, Alissa Quart discusses the rapid rise in the number of teenage girls undergoing cosmetic surgery to get bigger breasts, thinner thighs, smaller noses or plumper lips. She attributes this self-aversion to many factors, including the use of perfectly formed models to sell products and lifestyles. She points out the growing public acceptance, even glorification, of plastic surgery, with movie stars proudly showing off their altered bodies, and clients proudly posing for before-and-after shots. Some plastic surgeons are quick to exploit a teenager's self-contempt and Quart cites the example of a doctor whose website "offers up the profile of a fifteen-year-old as an inspiration to other girls with 'weak' chins and 'hook' noses."[1] Examples set by a teen's own mother can compound the problem. Quart speculates that teens and tweens may be particularly attracted to altering their bodies because they shift identity daily, and the idea of an overnight change has particular appeal.

Quart points out that young men are increasingly susceptible to similar pressures, and documents the astronomical rise in their use of steroids and nutritional supplements to increase athletic performance and build body mass. Vitamin products that target teens are fuelling this trend, a development that Quart calls "malignant genius." "There's nothing like a new teen-specific product," she says, "that claims to alleviate a new teen-specific pathology."[2] Teen magazines and websites support the rise of "bigorexia" by celebrating the look, and prescribing a strenuous exercise program and diet regime.

Emily saw the pressures first-hand when her son became a teenager. "I worried about my son when he was slightly overweight entering the teen years," she says, "and I watched him battle with body-image and self-esteem issues. I took a really low-key approach. I told him about some similar issues I had as a teen, but mostly I just stayed aware. I especially tried to be present and/or supportive when it came to 'revealing' experiences such as clothes shopping and swimming."

Shari Graydon's book *In Your Face: The Culture of Beauty and You* is an ideal primer for teens about the beauty industry. The book looks critically at the culture of beauty for both men and women, past and present, and provides critical tools such as reality checks and alternative beauty tips. Graydon includes a list of questions to ask yourself if you're considering self-improvement in whatever form, whether anti-cellulite cream, hair dye, protein supplements, surgery or a tattoo.

I asked Graydon for her advice to parents who are trying to support their teenager's positive body image and here's what she suggests. "Limit their exposure to media that make them feel bad about themselves—whether glamour magazines, music videos or fashion shows—so you're reducing the time they spend comparing themselves to some perceived unattainable perfection. For girls in particular, try and encourage them in some kind of physical activity that gives them an experience of what their bodies can do (shoot hoops, run hurdles) as opposed to what it looks like. It's important to be careful, though, about some activities, such as dance, diving and skating, where issues of body image can be problematic. Role modelling is critical. Moms who obsess about their own weight or make critical comments about the appearance of other women, such as female newscasters, help set up negative patterns. So do fathers who fixate on women's figures or men's 'pecs.' Praising and celebrating your children from a young age for attributes other than their appearance—such as their generosity, intelligence or courage—is important, especially if your teenager is constantly eliciting compliments from others on his or her beauty."

One way to approach these issues with your teen is to focus on the angle that they are being manipulated for commercial gain. Teenagers are particularly sensitive to being duped by the system, and there are several resources that can be effective tools for this discussion. The website www.plasticassets.com is a clever spoof that purports to offer free breast implants to anyone who signs up for a credit card, but is actually an educational site about the dangers of breast implants. Shari Graydon created the site in association with the Pantyraiders, a female-run collective who challenge media's conforming roles for women and sexuality.

Several websites offer teens the opportunity to talk back to the companies or advertisers whose messages contribute to negative body image. The website www.about-face.org includes a "gallery of offenders" containing negative and distorted images of women, and a "gallery of winners" with positive portrayals. There are ways to make your views known to the sources of these images—either with complaints or applause. The website http://loveyourbody.now foundation.org organizes events like the annual Love Your Body Day to encourage people to fight back against the cosmetics, fashion, magazine and diet-aids industries who profit from our insecurities. Adbusters Media Foundation provides more general resources for teens to become media savvy through campaigns like Buy Nothing Day and Digital Detox Week, organized through its magazine and website www.adbusters.org.

The KidsHealth website (see p. 265 for the URL) has a section for teens called "Help! Is This My Body?" that describes the various kinds of changes that can happen to teens' bodies when they hit puberty, and the impact this can have on how they feel about themselves. Examples include a young lean male athlete who becomes stockier with puberty, and a teenage dancer whose new curves mean she no longer fits the ballerina mould. The tips are good ones, including don't compare, forget magazine ads—check out family photos instead—befriend your body and walk tall, even if you're not.

The website of the National Eating Disorders Association (see p. 265 for the URL) reminds girls why every body is different and why ideal body weights vary. They are urged to list their own strengths instead of comparing themselves to others. The association's rules include respecting your body, fuelling it with a variety of foods and resisting the pressure to judge yourself and others based on weight, shape or size. Strategies for male eating disorders include tips to help boys see their body as a positive facet of their uniqueness and individuality. Advice includes finding friends who are not overly concerned about appearance, demonstrating respect for others who don't fit the ideal body type and becoming aware of your own negative messages about your self and your body.

Your teen might be intrigued by the Beautiful Women Project (see p. 265 for the URL), a collection of more than one hundred clay sculptures of frontal torsos of volunteers, aged nineteen to ninety-one. The artist, Cheryl-Ann Webster started casting real women after discovering that her thirteen-year-old daughter's friend was saving for breast implants "to get a better boyfriend." She's hoping that these examples of authentic beauty, rather than media-enhanced images, will convince young women they are beautiful just as they are, and raise awareness about the link between self-worth, self-identity and physical appearance.

Body Decoration vs. Body Mutilation

Today's online world exposures our teens to a galaxy of compelling images of rock stars, supermodels and athletic heroes who sport tattoos, tongue studs and body piercings. It is easy to dismiss our teenager's desire to decorate his body (or mutilate it, depending on your point of view) as a passing fad. But your child may feel that the only thing he has any control over is his body, and he's going to demonstrate that power through some form of body display. In many jurisdictions these procedures will not be performed on a minor without parental consent so, if your child is underage, one option is to just say "no." Helen said she simply used her "absolutely not" veto when her fourteen-year-old wanted a tongue piercing.

When we were confronted with a daughter who was set and determined to get a body piercing at age fourteen, we decided to support her, but we didn't make it easy. We decided against outright refusal for several reasons—she had persisted in her desire for many months and the issue seemed to be taking on an extreme importance; a couple of slightly older admired cousins had piercings done at the same age so it was hard to reject out-of-hand; and she was holding out for an okay from us even though some of her friends had already used forged documents to circumvent their parents' opposition. We decided to use the opportunity to model decision making by helping her understand both the health and safety aspects of her decision, as well as the long-term implications.

We explained that although her body was her own, any medical fallout from the procedure would have an impact on the whole family (e.g., if she contracted hepatitis from a dirty needle), so nothing could proceed unless her health was guaranteed. We asked her to do the following: contact our doctor to get a list of health and safety conditions that the tattoo/piercing parlour must meet, go with us to inspect the parlour beforehand, and interview other teens who had piercings from the same location to see whether there had been any complications. Oh, and one last thing—she had to agree there would be no more body mutilation until she was eighteen (by which point we hoped most of this would have blown over!). We advised her to pierce the part of her body that would have the lowest impact on her future options. What would she do if a prospective employer didn't like her lip ring; what if she grew tired of the nose stud and the opening never healed over completely; what if the tongue stud ruined her orthodontic work? We encouraged her to research these questions.

Our list of requirements would have put off all but the most determined, and it did give her pause—but only for a few months. She eventually did meet all the conditions and had her belly button pierced in a downtown tattoo parlour, with me watching. Her father was waiting in a nearby

coffee shop. He had started out with us at the tattoo parlour but made the mistake of flipping through their portfolio of piercings. As he turned green, our daughter
remarked, "I don't think Dad's going to make it." As he left
the building, I reminded my daughter, "You have to give
your dad full credit—he's spent fourteen years protecting
you from harm and now he's standing by while you're deliberately allowing yourself to be hurt." Over a decade later
she says she still likes her belly-button piercing, and it has
never given her any problems. She adds, "More importantly, looking back, I feel that my piercings made me more
accepting of my body at a time when I was having body-
image issues."

Cosmetic procedures have risks, and as guardians of our
teen's welfare we have an obligation to make sure they are
fully aware of the medical and career implications of body
decoration. Websites with doctor-approved resources can
help you negotiate this terrain with your teen. The teen
section at www.kidshealth.org has a useful item under Body
Art with the procedures for body piercing and tattooing
described in clinical detail, and an emphasis on doing the
research and taking the steps to keep yourself healthy. A
checklist itemizes what you need to look for to ensure that
the procedure is safe and sanitary. A section on after-effects
includes descriptions of temporary symptoms as well as signs
that something more serious has gone wrong.

My daughter says she was completely turned off tongue
studs by the full-colour photo I showed her from the local
newspaper of the shaved, scarred head of a teenager whose

tongue piercing had turned into a brain infection. Similarly, I have told my daughters that some anesthesiologists are refusing to give epidurals during childbirth to women who have lower-back tattoos for fear of infection.[3] Whether or not this is a reasonable action on the part of the doctors, we need to warn our daughters. How awful if they were denied pain relief in the middle of a difficult labour because of a trendy tattoo that seemed so harmless at the time.

Howard Bargman, a professor of Dermatology at the University of Toronto, specializes in laser treatment and has removed many tattoos over the years. He writes, "I have seen infections, allergic reactions, migration of tattoo ink and discontent with the appearance of the tattoo." He reports that studies indicate that 50 percent of people eventually wish that they did not have their tattoo, and he urges people to consider the downside before proceeding.[4]

Smoke-Free vs. Nicotine-Addicted

On the website of The Foundation for a Smokefree America (see p. 265 for the URL), you'll find a compelling anti-smoking message for teenagers from Patrick Reynolds. Reynolds is a grandson of the founder of the R. J. Reynolds Tobacco Company and himself a former pack-a-day smoker. After watching his father, oldest brother and other relatives die from cigarette-induced emphysema, heart disease and cancer, he set up the foundation and decided to devote his life to achieving a smoke-free society, and to motivating young people to stay tobacco-free.

Reynolds tells youth how easy it is to get hooked on smoking and emphasizes what their addiction will cost them. He cites a study showing that one quarter of eleven- to thirteen-year-olds who smoked as few as two or three cigarettes a day became addicted in just two weeks, and that many of the rest got addicted shortly after that. He reminds them that, once hooked, the average smoker is unable to stop for seventeen years. The financial argument Reynolds makes is probably even more persuasive to a teenager. If teen smokers saved their money rather than wasting it on cigarettes, after only two years they could have enough to buy their first car.

When Carol's daughter started smoking at age thirteen, she used the indirect approach. "The first time I realized that my daughter had been smoking, I said, 'Shannon, you really smell like cigarette smoke. People will think you've been smoking—and you know people can always tell, because you can smell it a mile away.' She mumbled something about being in a store with cigarette smoke, and that was the end of it. I don't think she did it again. If I had confronted her on it, I think she might well have taken up smoking just to make the point. I found an indirect approach often worked best because then they weren't put in the position either of denying what they'd done, or feeling they had to defend their 'right' to do something. For most teenagers, fighting back and resisting seems to be the default mode."

We found our heavy-handed efforts to get our daughter to quit smoking totally ineffective; in fact, they may have backfired. Because I have lost several dear friends to early deaths from smoking-related lung cancer, the issue is emotionally charged for me. So when my daughter began smoking at age fifteen, I could barely contain my anguish and anxiety. She knew of my concern and never smoked in front of me, but kept smoking with her friends. I kept giving her articles on lung cancer and on nicotine's powerfully addictive qualities, along with offers of programs to help her quit.

Our most blatant intervention came when a close friend, who was suffering from melanoma, asked my daughter to accompany her to the cancer ward for her treatment. While there my friend recounted the story of her brother, who had died of HIV/AIDS and who wanted passionately to live. She told my daughter how angry he was at a friend of his who had committed suicide. She said, "That's how I feel about you and your smoking." As my friend tells the story, tears came into my daughter's eyes and my friend felt everyone in the waiting room look accusingly at her for making this sweet girl cry. She immediately felt guilty—even though she meant every word. When my daughter came home and berated me for "setting her up," I replied, "You're lucky someone cares enough about you to even try."

Now looking back as a young adult, my daughter says she felt betrayed by the hospital incident. She still gets angry thinking about it and says, "It was totally inappropriate." She says there is nothing we can do to help her quit smoking before she is good and ready. Once that day comes, if she wants help, I'll suggest she go to http://smokefree.gov, an online guide to quitting smoking including links by phone and instant messaging to supportive experts. The website is full of helpful resources, including links to cessation studies on the effectiveness of prescription and other non-nicotine methods.

Drinking vs. Alcoholism

With young people posting online photos celebrating themselves and their friends in advanced states of inebriation, we shouldn't be surprised if our teens think it's cool to be drunk. For many parents drinking is an ongoing issue during the teen years and research findings confirm our concerns that our teenagers need to get their drinking under control. According to the journal *Archives of Pediatric & Adolescent Medicine*, fourteen- to nineteen-year-olds who drink are 45 percent more likely to become alcohol-dependent later in age than those who start drinking after the age of twenty. And 70 to 80 percent of people who are dependent on alcohol as adults started off with heavy alcohol consumption in adolescence.[5]

Alcohol became a battleground for Debbie and her sons once they became teenagers. "They spent Friday and Saturday nights with friends," she explains, "and it wasn't long before we became aware that drinking was part of it, starting at age fifteen and becoming more obvious at sixteen. We invited our sons to have a beer with Dad, or wine with dinner, but there was no interest whatsoever. The drinking had nothing to do with liking beer, and everything to do with peer acceptance. We had set up a great basement hangout with pool table, entertainment centre, etcetera, because we wanted the kids to bring friends home. As soon as we realized that sixteen-year-olds were downstairs drinking, we put the kibosh on it and—guess what? No kids. They just went somewhere else. This happened with both our sons. When we relented to one beer at age seventeen they all came back, en masse. The most nerve-racking years were when they were in their late seventeens into eighteens. These kids drank a lot, and we knew if anything happened as a result of drinking at our house we were responsible. We also knew they were going to drink no matter what. None of the kids would drink and drive, but there are plenty of other things that can happen when young people get drunk, and we talked to our boys a lot about this. In retrospect, I think we may just as well have saved our breath."

Dr. John Knight of the Center for Adolescent Substance Abuse Research at Children's Hospital Boston created a website (see p. 265 for the URL) to emphasize the dangers posed by alcoholism to our teens and to provide advice on how to keep them safe. The site includes questions from parents with answers provided by Dr. Knight, including "What do I do when my teen comes home drunk?", "Doesn't my teen need to drink to be popular?" and "How do I keep my kid safe at the after-prom party?"

One way to get your teen to focus on his level of alcohol consumption is to suggest he take a ten-minute confidential online survey found at www.checkyourdrinking.net. When he finishes answering the questions he will receive a report that compares his weekly consumption with others in his age range. The report estimates the amount of money he spent on alcohol and the number of calories he consumed, and charts the likelihood he will have problems in the other parts of his life because of his drinking. John A. Cunningham, a professor of social and behavioural sciences at the University of Toronto, developed the survey and has found that problem drinkers who took the survey cut their drinking by about a third.[6]

As an older teen, my daughter had high praise for the website www.factsontap.org with its section called Transitions, a prevention program for college-bound high-school students. Its matter-of-fact tone treats drugs and alcohol as an integral part of your teen's new independence, and provides sound advice on living responsibly within the new-found freedoms. The section for parents is equally practical and realistic in its approach, and reminds us that parents still matter, even at this age, and that our influence and advice do make a difference.

Jane found that acceptance (and laughter) helped her son learn to establish his own limits around alcohol. "Ryan says he grew up when it came to booze because of the way I handled his first, and last, alcohol overdose. He came home so drunk one night that he vomited several times at the side of his bed. I nursed him through it with noodle soup. I laughed at his non-stop talking (when he wasn't hurling) and hugged him. He says he knew from then on that he never had to hide anything from me about drinking, and that he had to put controls on himself."

One way to start a conversation with your teenagers about the potentially humiliating consequences of excess drinking is to tell them Melody's story. "When my son was seventeen years old," she recalls, "he invited a girl who was a friend to be his date for the big dance. A party at somebody's house preceded the dance, and the drinking started there. According to my son, everyone was drinking, but it hit the girls harder, because they'd been starving themselves to fit into their dresses. So before they'd even left the party, my son's friend was holed up in the washroom, semi-comatose, slumped over the toilet bowl in her beautiful dress with her girlfriends holding her head while she puked. My son was terrified, and decided that he had better protect her from any repercussions by sneaking her into her house before her parents, who were out for the evening, were any the wiser. So, they couldn't join the others in the shared limousine that was heading for the dance (which had cost more than his allowance). And he scraped together enough money for a cab to her house. When the cab arrived he struggled to get her into the back seat. I remember vividly his description of what happened when they got to her home. 'Mom, it was really awful. I could barely get her out of the cab, and I had to put her on the ground in her beautiful dress so I could pay the driver. Her boobs fell out of her top and I didn't want the driver to see so I had to push them back in.' He eventually got her into her house, and then walked all the way home. As he told me this story about why he had missed the dance, I had to contain my laughter and keep a straight face. Somehow the two of them remained friends, and I have to assume that there were some lessons learned!"

Getting High vs. Getting Hooked

Cellphones give drug dealers easy access to our teens and make it child's play to place orders and organize deliveries. They also make it easy for our children to become drug dealers. And if our teens want to experiment with a do-it-yourself approach, a quick website search will take them to sites offering step-by-step instructions for making drugs like crystal meth (one of the street names used for methamphetamine). Fortunately, the online world also gives parents and teens the tools to become forewarned and forearmed.

Parent Action on Drugs was launched by a group of concerned parents and emphasizes parent-teen dialogue. The organization stresses prevention by helping teens make informed choices, and begins by focusing on the parents. PAD programs are designed to give parents ways to talk to their children about drugs and to identify problems before they become serious. They also offer counselling, including telephone support and referrals, for parents who have concerns about their child's use of drugs.

The website www.childrennow.org has a section on "Talking with kids about tough issues," which includes a very helpful tip sheet for talking to your children about drugs, including advice such as getting the facts about the substances your teen may be using, looking at life through your child's eyes, and practising what you preach. Another source of information and advice is found at www.theanti-drug.com, where you can find everything from the characteristics of specific drugs to real teen stories of addiction and drug abuse. An e-monitoring tutorial helps you understand the technologies that are second nature to your child so that you can be more vigilant about their activities. You can also subscribe to a parenting tips newsletter. The National Institute on Drug Abuse (NIDA) created a website (see p. 266 for the URL) to educate teens from eleven through fifteen, as well as their parents and teachers, on the science behind drug abuse. NIDA enlisted the help of teens in developing the site, which uses animated illustrations, quizzes and games to deliver science-based facts about how drugs affect the brain and body. Another website for teens is www.justthinktwice.com run by the U.S. Drug Enforcement Administration. A section called "It Can't Happen to Me" covers topics such as "Your Brain Changes from Drugs," "Your Friend ODs," "Your Drink Is Drugged" and "You Are High and Drive."

Many teenagers experiment with drugs, whether marijuana, hallucinogenic drugs or stimulants. If you're lucky, they won't like the experience and that will be the end of it. My daughter says she was decidedly uncomfortable with the feeling of lack of control that accompanied her drug experimentations. She decided that she "didn't do drugs," and was supported in her choice when a hip drug-using friend told her admiringly that her decision was "cool." I am forever grateful to this unknown young man because his words were much more effective than mine could ever have been. I did extract an agreement from my daughters that they would never put a pill in their mouth if they didn't know what it contained, which covered anything they might be handed. I supported my request with graphic descriptions worthy of a forensic investigator of the disgusting things that could happen to their body and the horrifying pain they might have to endure if the unknown pill were to contain a substance such as rat poison. Their schools seemed to have been even more effective at "grossing them out" with scare-tactic videos, and my daughter still remembers vividly the close-ups of track marks on the arms of wasted heroin addicts.

But these worlds can seem to have no connection to the backyard where your teen is having fun smoking weed with his or her friends. My friend Campbell started smoking marijuana when he was twelve and then it was only occasionally, for fun. But he remembers that he really started using dope when he was fifteen, and that his life started to spin out of control. "I figure I was smoking fifteen to twenty-five hours a week, and drinking alcohol on top of it," he remembers. Looking back, he feels that he was using drugs to ease the pain of an undiagnosed major depressive disorder. But his self-medication started causing its own symptoms. "The drug use became a Catch-22 because it only exaggerated my problems, and I soon became a burnout, and was left with few friends." Campbell eventually suffered a nervous breakdown brought on by a bout of heatstroke combined with heavy drug use. "I decided this was the last straw and I went cold turkey. It took several months before I was 'normal' again." His depressive condition was subsequently diagnosed and successfully treated with medication and cognitive behavioural therapy.

Campbell is now a vibrant, engaged young man in his twenties for whom "life has never been better," and I asked him what advice he had for parents who suspect their teens are smoking dope. "If you are honest and respectful with your sons and daughters," he says, "they will respond in kind. Respect creates an aura of trust that ensures your children know they are not submissive subjects in the house, but respected peers. If you suspect that your teen is using drugs and alcohol, don't put him down, don't harass him, and don't ever act like you have never been there yourself. Looking down on your teenager will only antagonize the situation and create a rift. Gently approach your son or daughter and ask them if they are using. Enforce the idea that you care about them enough to ask them. Sharing some of your stories may help, depending on the situation, but there is a danger this approach might seem tacky and detached, as well as cliché. Honesty and openness is the key. Talk *with* them, not *at* them."

But in order to implement Campbell's advice we first have to recognize the problem, and, for that, we need to be paying careful attention. Teens can be very clever at covering up. Helen's daughter wore coloured contact lens to disguise her drug use: "The tinted glass hid her dilated pupils so it took me a lot longer to catch on," she says.

Eating vs. Controlling

Eating disorders such as anorexia or bulimia are affecting both teenage boys and girls in record numbers. The online world is aggravating the problem with "pro-ana" websites (i.e., pro-anorexia) that increase your teen's medical risk by encouraging a sense of community among anorexics and glorifying the disease. They feature dangerously skinny models for "thinspiration" and offer tips on how to be a more successful anorexic (e.g., how to hide your vomiting and suppress your hunger). Medical studies such as those published in the *International Journal of Eating Disorders* confirm that these sites are dangerous, and that your teen's participation in the pro-ana websites is a cause for concern.

The experts feel that teenagers are particularly vulnerable to eating disorders because the dysfunction is more about control than about food. Teenagers often feel that their lives are run by other people, and the only thing they can control is their bodies. So they exercise power over themselves through food, particularly at times when they are feeling most powerless. Alissa Quart, in her book *Branded: The Buying and Selling of Teenagers*, quotes a number of anorexic young women who explain that anorexia makes them feel good about themselves because they set "thinness goals" and achieve them. They then feel special because "I have more control over myself than anybody else."[7] But anorexia is not a lifestyle choice; it is a serious medical condition and, along with other eating disorders, requires treatment.

So how do we know when our teenager's concerns about weight and body shape have turned into an eating disorder? The National Eating Disorder Information Centre (see

p. 266 for the URL) says you need to be concerned if the way your teen eats and thinks about food interferes with his or her life, and keeps him or her from enjoying life and moving forward. Their website has an Eating Disorder Self-Check to help in this determination, as well as a resource library with a range of useful information about getting and giving help.

"My son struggled with anorexia in his early teens," Catherine says. "He lost about thirty-five pounds over a period of three or four months. He had been chubby, but not overweight, and now he was over six feet tall and very thin. I recognized the symptoms because I had been anorexic as a thirteen-year-old. I told him this and warned him that it was a dangerous disease and he needed to take it very seriously. I told him I thought my anorexia was caused by a fear of loss of my childhood and a need to control something about myself. He read me a poem he had written in which he described the incredible feeling you get when you stop eating and weight falls off and you feel so powerful. This really worried me so I took him to our pediatrician. The doctor agreed that his rapid weight loss was concerning, and asked him many questions about how he had lost the weight, whether he exercised, etcetera. He warned him that if he continued to lose weight, he would advise us not to allow him to go to summer camp, and I should bring him back in a month to be weighed. When I did, his weight had stabilized, so he was allowed to go to camp. For about a year, I kept watching his weight, but the phase had passed. He is still slender, but healthy."

The National Eating Disorders Association (see p. 266 for the URL) is dedicated to expanding public understanding of eating disorders. It promotes access to quality treatment for those affected, along with support for their families through education, advocacy and research. Resources include stories of hope from people who have recovered from eating disorders. A downloadable Parent Toolkit has information on eating disorder signs, symptoms and behaviour, and treatment options. The National Association of Anorexia Nervosa and Associated Disorders (see p. 266 for the URL) is a thirty-year-old non-profit organization that acts as a resource centre about eating disorders, including sources and facilities for treatment.

Helping Your Teenager Beat an Eating Disorder, by James Lock and Daniel Le Grange, describes the havoc eating disorders can wreak on the family. The book emphasizes the importance of the role of parents in the healing process and offers troubleshooting tools. Other recommended reading can be found on the website for Sheena's Place (see p. 266 for the URL), a centre providing support programs for people with eating disorders and their families.

Physical Fitness vs. Body Abuse

Parents have always worried about the health of their teenagers and now, with the digital world, we have a whole new slew of problems. For example, when we tell our teens they're going to be deafened if they keep blasting their eardrums with their iPod, we're right. A study published by the American Medical Association found that teen hearing loss is up 30 percent over testing done a decade earlier. Another study done by the Hearing Foundation of Canada found that 30 percent of teens in their survey exposed themselves to noise at levels and durations that were hazardous.[8] "I find myself continually warning my teens about the dangers of playing their music at a decibel level that can cause hearing damage," Marilyn says. "My rule is that if I can hear the music from their earbuds, the volume is way too loud and must be turned down. But to use a metaphor that they wouldn't even understand anymore, I am a broken record on this one."

And then there's cellphone radiation, which has been linked to brain cancer. While the evidence is inconclusive, there's no point in taking chances. In *Disconnect*, Devra Davis, a scientist who has studied the problem, recommends that children text instead of speaking on their cellphone, and limit phone use to emergencies. For those who need their cellphones to function, she recommends the use of headsets and digital gadgets such as Bluetooth to reduce the level of radiation. According to her advice, our teens should store their cellphones in a backpack or purse, not on their person, sleep with their cellphone nowhere near them, and talk only in areas with good reception since poor reception requires the phone to power up and emit more radiation. Davis herself uses her cellphone cautiously, and then only while using a headset.[9]

Repetitive strain injury is another side effect of the digital world. My friend Liz, the one I told you about earlier who removed *Solitaire* and *Sudoku* from her iPhone, found that her obsessive game-playing, coupled with constant texting, gave her a repetitive strain injury from the continual use of her thumbs. "I asked my physiotherapist what I could do to help the pain in my arm," she said. "His response was, 'Stop texting!' So now I give myself 'texting-free' days." Liz's injury reminded me of a very sad phone conversation I had with a tech support person who apologized for typing slowly. "I'm learning how to type with only my left hand," he explained, "because I've damaged my right one from years on this job." I asked him what he was going to do after his left hand had become damaged as well. He replied, "Guess I'll start on my feet!" We need to teach our teens to be proactive about combatting the effects of excessive computer use before things reach this stage, and some relief can be found online. For example, YouTube videos provide suggested exercises such as a Repetitive Strain Injury Exercise Program.[10]

The endless hours sitting in front of the computer mean that our teens are not getting enough exercise nor taking the time to eat properly. About a third of our young people are overweight from a combination of poor nutrition and lack of physical activity, and the situation is getting worse.[11] In the past twenty years, obesity rates in children and adolescents have almost tripled in the United States, Canada and Britain, and we need to be concerned about helping our teens maintain a healthy weight. Here are some of the problems overweight children may face: increased risk of diabetes, cardiovascular disease, back problems, osteoarthritis and some cancers, as well as newly discovered links between obesity and girls' infertility.[12]

From the time our daughters were young, I took the position that weight alone is a poor measure of physical health. Instead of weighing themselves obsessively, I urged them to concentrate on eating well and exercising. I reinforced the message by not having a scale in our house. I said that they would know how fit they were by how they felt and how much energy they had. I explained that when I was in high school the heaviest girl I knew was also the fittest because she was a gymnast and her body was pure muscle. At the same time, I knew that if we parents obsessed about our own weight, it would be tough to send a different message to our children. So my husband and I made sure that any issues around our own fitness were not couched in terms of calories.

This approach worked pretty well when our daughters were young. Physical fitness was a family activity that included regular weekends at the gym where the girls swam, and played squash and badminton while we exercised. When the girls weren't at summer camp, family holidays were spent sailing, canoeing and skiing. But once the girls became teens, whatever good habits we thought we had instilled fell by the wayside. They participated in some team sports at school, but they both dropped phys. ed as a school subject just as soon as it was no longer mandatory. With one daughter, I conspired with the parents of her two best friends to get them memberships at the YMCA. We imagined them meeting other teenagers, working out and taking dance and hip-hop classes. For a while the three of them regularly headed off with their gym bags, and the plan seemed to have worked—or so we thought. My daughter now confesses that when they said they were "going to the Y" this was only a "technical truth." The three of them would sit in the lobby and talk, and then go off to eat Chinese food at a nearby restaurant. What an eloquent reminder this is of the truism "you can bring a horse to water but you can't make it drink." The other daughter only rediscovered the gym at the age of eighteen. She credits her first-year university friends for transforming her from what she calls her "lazy self" to someone who loves eating nutritious food and being fit. Because her friends are "crazy active" and love the outdoors, they've gotten her hooked.

Thinking back on their teenage years, both daughters say they are grateful we never owned a scale. My daughter said that she was filling out a form recently, and when it came to the space to record her weight she realized she had absolutely no idea what she weighed. She had to ask a similarly sized friend what *she* weighed and use that as a proxy. She admitted there were a couple of times in her early teens when she would hop onto scales in the bathrooms of other people's homes, but she gradually lost interest. Both of them feel that the absence of a scale in the house did reduce the number of times during their teen years when they were preoccupied with thoughts of pounds and calories.

I suggested my daughter see a naturopath when she was in her mid-teens and began to complain of headaches and lack of energy. From that visit she learned about the impact her high-sugar, high-caffeine diet was having on her health and well-being. The next day we bought countless varieties of caffeine-free teas and coffees, and I thought that her eating habits were changed by the advice. She's less convinced than I am that the visit was decisive and feels it's only the healthy habits of her current peer group that are making a difference in her diet and exercise program. Nevertheless, I recommend the use of naturopaths and nutritionists as another way to help our teenagers break the vicious cycle of seeing food only as weight-bearing calories, rather than as fuel to power a healthy mind and body. It does matter what you eat and sometimes professionals can communicate this more effectively than parents.

And while we're on the subject of caffeine, the age of coffee drinkers is falling while the level of consumption is rising, and the use of caffeine-laden energy drinks by teenagers is widespread. If your teenager complains of headaches, anxiety, insomnia, digestive problems, or heart palpitations, have a look at his caffeine intake. The U.S. National Institute of Mental Health reports that teachers found eight- to thirteen-year-olds who regularly consumed high doses of caffeine to be more restless than their non-caffeinated colleagues. One-third of the caffeine-consuming children met the criteria for attention deficit hyperactivity disorder (ADHD).[13]

If you want to turn your teens off junk food completely, giving them the book *Chew On This: Everything You Don't Want to Know About Fast Food* might just do the trick.

Written for teenagers by Eric Schlosser and Charles Wilson, the book reveals what's really in the food we eat, and why teens are highly valued customers for the fast-food industry. Reading the book will probably make them feel nauseated, but more importantly, it should make them feel duped. The book is particularly successful at showing how teens are targeted by the fast-food industry through locking up the contracts in their school cafeterias and by advertising on their TV shows.

At the same time the digital world is bringing new health challenges, it is providing tools that might inspire our teens to adopt healthy behaviours. A variety of smart-phone applications help users become proactive about their health, including *Tap & Track*, an all in one app for diet and exercise and *iTreadmill*, a pedometer that selects a tune with matching beat once you've established your stride. For teens with diabetes there are a number of apps to assist them with disease management including *Glucose Buddy*, *Diabetes Diary* and *Livestrong*, which focuses on nutrition. Toronto's Hospital for Sick Children (SickKids) is developing a more in-depth iPhone app to help a group of patients twelve to fifteen years of age with type 1 diabetes manage their condition. The app is designed with teens in mind and includes iTunes redemption codes for taking their readings regularly.[14]

The Teen-Parent Connection

Communicating vs. Texting

S PEAKING WITH PARENTS, I found the overriding and preoccupying issue was how to understand what was going on with their teenagers. This was no doubt true when we were teenagers but the problem seems to be exacerbated by the amount of time our children are spending in cyberspace. We desperately want to know what is on their minds—what is worrying them, what is making them sad, what is making them happy. But once our children hit puberty many of them, especially boys, stop talking (at least, to us), and we struggle to find ways to draw them out. Paradoxically the digital world can help us feel closer physically to our teens, but farther away psychologically. Our son sits next to us on the sofa but won't talk to us because he's on the Internet; our daughter calls us on her cellphone to tell us where she is, but she's actually somewhere other than she claims; we're gathered around the dinner table as a family, but the teens are texting under the table rather than joining the conversation.

Text messaging is a perfect example of the fine line between connecting and communicating. Marilyn uses texting to stay in touch with her four children, three of whom are teenagers. "Texting is a godsend," she says. "My kids often won't respond to a phone call, but get right back to a text message. They'll send me a text late at night to say where they are and I often text them even when they're in the house to tell them to come to the dinner table." Texting is quick, cheaper than a cellphone call, your message can be received even in a noisy venue, and it allows for more privacy. And if your teen is too embarrassed to answer your phone call in front of her friends, she might respond to a quick text query.[1]

But as terrific as texting can be for quickly touching base, it is tough to use for more sensitive topics or difficult issues. At times like these, we need other techniques, and parents need to be very inventive. Helen used the book, *Yes, Your Parents Are Crazy!: A Teen Survival Guide*, as her mouthpiece when her daughter Erin was late coming home from school one day. Helen had purchased the book for Erin when she found the two of them were having real problems communicating. When Helen picked the book off the shelf at the bookstore Erin wanted to know why Helen chose that book rather than its companion *Yes, Your Teen Is Crazy!* Helen replied, "I know what's going on in your head, but you don't have a clue what's going on in mine.

Please read this." The book proved its value late one winter day when Erin wasn't home from school when she should have been and it was already pitch black. What really set Helen off were the warnings of a sexual predator on the prowl in their neighbourhood. "When Erin finally got home I was frantic with worry," Helen remembers, "and I met her at the door in an apoplectic rage. I completely lost it! And, of course, Erin responded in kind and rushed to her room and slammed her door. So after I calmed down, I realized I had blown it. I found the book and turned to the chapter on missed curfews, and, sure enough, there I was—described perfectly—having a fit. But the beauty of the book was that it was able to explain, in a way I couldn't right at that moment, what had happened to me. My mommy brain had immediately leapt to the worst-case scenario—hence the fear and the rage. Erin read it and shrugged, but I could see that she got it."

Some parents recommend putting your thoughts down on paper, or in an e-mail, and saying to your teen, "Read this and then we'll talk." The process of writing this book provided opportunities for this kind of dialogue. Many of the contributors, including me, showed their teenagers the stories they had written and the exercise became a catalyst for some important discussions. You'll see an example in the section "Curfew vs. Power Struggle" on page 215, where Jane and her son David debate what she wrote about handling his curfew.

Ashley, who is seventeen years old, says that the mother/daughter book club she and her mother attend is an excellent communication tool. "The books raise so many topics we wouldn't necessarily think of talking about with our moms, and we feel comfortable since we're with our friends. And the moms are relaxed because they're having fun, too. So it's a great way to really discuss things, maybe get certain subjects out in the open, and hear the different points of view."

One favourite technique to get your teen talking is to drive them around. But the deal is this: to get the ride, they have to unplug from their digital devices. On the face of it, giving your children a lift when they're old enough to walk, take a bus or even drive themselves may seem to foster dependency, encourage laziness or deprive them of good exercise. But parents say that what you gain in personal connection is worth the downsides. As Carol says, "Taking opportunities for conversation during travel in cars, preferably in the dark, often works well. You are both captive—can't walk (or stomp) upstairs when it gets difficult. You can avoid eye contact. And it somehow gives a safe—and private—venue for talking."

Driving your teen and his friends around is also a good way to learn about his life. When you're driving a car full of teenagers they usually forget you're there, and you're provided with an ethical way of eavesdropping. One car ride of spontaneous conversation can tell you a lot and the intelligence can come in handy when you're trying to intercept problems later on (e.g., Q: "But isn't Randy the one whose licence is suspended?" A: "Mom, who told you that?").

Another recommended strategy, even though it's hard to pull off in today's busy world, is the family dinner. Research done since 1996 by the National Center on Addiction and Substance Abuse at Columbia University has consistently found that family dinners have a positive effect on both a child's social development and on the cohesiveness of the family. "Dinner was the time," says Maria, "when we all came together and nobody was allowed to miss dinner without a good reason. On Sundays, our extended family—aunts, uncles, and cousins—joined us. We often had our children's friends at the table, too, and it was a good way to get to know them. Sometimes the conversations got heated, sometimes there was a lot of laughter, and sometimes nobody had much to say, but we were all together. For me, meal time was when I read the pulse of my teens."

To help get a reading of the teenage pulse, as Maria so aptly puts it, we established a ritual of sharing stories around the dinner table during special holidays. At Thanksgiving each of us talks about something for which we want to give thanks and then everyone else has a chance to give their own opinions about why the speaker should be grateful. The New Year's topic is "the best thing and the worse thing that happened to me this year," followed by everyone else's assessment of your year. As you can imagine, the practice makes for much hilarity, as well as some real insights into our daughters' worlds. When friends participate they make some wonderfully insightful observations about the girls, which often has more impact than anything we parents might have said.

Helen found that the key to getting her teenagers to engage in dinner conversation was to focus on issues and opinions, rather than plying them with personal questions. "We used mealtime discussions about events at school, in the community, and around the world to help them develop a sense of values," she says. "We asked them, 'What do you think?', 'Why would you do that?', 'What would you do differently?', 'What's important to you?' We also used events in our adult lives to teach by example. We tried to impart to our children that they have to develop a set of principles and values to live by. We explained why our principles led us to treat someone a certain way, or how our actions were based on our values. Around the dinner table is the very best place to teach this to children from the earliest age possible."

But don't despair if these idealized meal times are not happening regularly in your home. Even watching TV together while you chow down may be enough to convey a sense of togetherness. Research indicates that it's the dedicated time that you're able to spend with your teen, when you're not on the BlackBerry and when he's not texting, that can be a powerful form of communicating and connecting.[2]

One way to open up lines of communication with your teen is to enter their domain and join them in playing video games. Constance Steinkuehler, assistant professor of Educational Communication and Technology at the University of Wisconsin-Madison, recommends this. "It's a really powerful way for parents and children to get in the same space," she says, "and literally remove all of that baggage of 'I'm your parent, and you're the child, and I'm the authority.' It troubles it up when your kid can outgame you, but it's a lot of fun."[3]

For a good barometer of your teen's attitudes and viewpoints, Joan recommends watching TV together. "You can find out a lot about what is going on in your teen's life by listening to what she has to say about the shows," she says. "My daughter and I have watched everything from the Disney and Family channel shows to *Teen Mom* and *Dog the Bounty Hunter*. Almost every one of them generates an opportunity for discussion, from simply distinguishing between reality and TV to issues raised in the shows, from the appropriateness of the solutions from our respective viewpoints to whether Dog's son Leland is 'hot.'"

Movies can be another tool for communicating with your teenager. One movie recommended to me by a therapist is *Thirteen*, directed by Catherine Hardwicke and written by Hardwicke and Nikki Reed. Reed was thirteen years of age when she co-wrote the script. As Hardwicke says in the DVD, "Nikki and I did the script writing in six days and then she went back to the eighth grade." The Oscar-nominated movie follows Tracy, a thirteen-year-old girl (Evan Rachael Wood) as she falls under the spell of a cool but toxic best friend (Reed) and discovers shoplifting, body piercing, sex and drugs. Tracy will do anything to become part of Reed's "in crowd," and she lives every parent's worst nightmare as she goes from being a good girl to a bad girl almost overnight. The mother (Holly Hunter) loves her daughter and watches the transformation with shock and disbelief as she tries to stave off disaster.

Hardwicke was inspired to make the film because of her concern over what was happening to her friend Nikki once she became a teenager. As she says on the DVD, "I met Nikki when she was five. She was the daughter of family friends. When she turned twelve or thirteen there were some major changes—she was angry at her mom and dad, and angry at the world. She was obsessed with her hair and would wake up at 4:30 A.M. so she could put on her make-up just to go to seventh grade. I wanted to get her into creative stuff rather than destructive stuff. So we talked about writing a teen comedy together, but it didn't turn out that funny. We based the script on what was happening to her and her friends, and it turned out to be much more interesting than anything we could have made up."[4]

Hardwicke and the teenage cast hope that parents will watch the movie with their teenagers and use it as a provocation and a conversation starter. They hope parents will see the kinds of pressures their kids are under and urge them to be open-minded. They also argue that schools should get more money for the arts, and kids should be given creative things to do. Parents should note that the movie has an R rating for "drug use, self-destructive violence, language and sexuality, all involving young teens."

Family meetings work well for some families, but not for others. Emily's family used meetings as a forum where she and her husband could discuss issues with their two sons, and communicate their values and expectations. "We wanted to make sure that everyone, at the very least, knew what behaviours were completely unacceptable (e.g., dealing drugs, drinking and driving, smoking cigarettes). Curfews and amount of 'screen time' have been issues with each of our sons. We used the occasional family meeting to review and/or set new limits. These meetings have often been heated, but always ended up with negotiated settlements that the boys have understood and respected. Sometimes this involved consultation with other families to see what the 'norm' was."

In contrast, Pat says that meetings never worked for her family. Any time they tried to use a formal meeting to discuss issues with their teenage daughter, the tensions that developed between father and daughter made the exercise counterproductive. "Now we don't even try holding family meetings. Kathy gets incredibly frustrated with her father in those situations. It's just the way it's always been. Aren't family dynamics interesting?" Instead of family meetings they use a dry-erase board with great effectiveness, as described below.

Parents stress the importance of developing techniques to communicate the whereabouts of *all* the family members—not just the teenagers. The underlying message is that we all matter to one another, and it's important that we know how to reach one another. People use a variety of methods including calendars, bulletin boards and sticky notes.

Marilyn's family tapes stuff on the fridge or on the front door, if it's something that came up on short notice. I was always careful to note my own whereabouts on our calendar and bulletin board, and asked our daughters to do the same. I explained that it wasn't a matter of control. I wanted to be able to reach them in the case of emergency because

I might need their help. It always made me sad when I would remind a visiting teen to be sure to let her parents know where she was, only to be told, "They don't care where I am."

Pat uses a dry-erase board for family communications, along with a large monthly calendar. "My husband, our teenage daughter Kathy and I all use the board to leave notes for each other and reminders about what's coming up or that the dog hasn't been walked. I use it to let them know I love them when I leave town for a few days (and to remind them to feed the dog!). We sometimes do doodlings with our notes, like I'll say 'went swimming' and draw a person swimming. Also, it's to leave phone messages. So it's used for both mundane reminders as well as important personal communications, about half and half. There's usually something written on it." And the board proved to be invaluable when Kathy missed her curfew, as Pat describes in the next section.

Regardless of the technique we use to communicate with our teen, we need to ground it with genuine and unconditional love. Neufeld and Maté say that we need to express our delight in our child's very being. "There are thousands of ways this invitation can be conveyed: in gesture, in words, in symbols, and in actions. The child must know that she is wanted, special, significant, valued, appreciated, missed, and enjoyed."[5]

Curfew vs. Power Struggle

Curfews can pose daily struggles for families with teens, and the digital world has added another layer of complexity. Teens will argue that we don't need to know where they are going or when they'll be home because we can always reach them on their cellphones. But cellphones run out of battery charge or break down, or they can be lost or stolen. Or our teen may decide not to answer. And then there are the deliberate falsehoods. Marilyn recalls the time her son called to say that he was staying for dinner at his girlfriend's house. "In fact," she says, "the two of them were in our garage, where they had been, shall we say, 'privately engaged.' I had my antenna twitching and when he called back a moment later and asked to speak to his brother I made sure I could overhear their conversation. He was asking his brother to distract me so that he and his girlfriend could slip unseen down the driveway!"

Pat tells a story of the time her daughter didn't call when expected and a "dead" cellphone added to her anxiety. "One night when Kathy was fifteen, she was working after school at a restaurant. She usually called us at 10:30 P.M., when the restaurant closed. This time she hadn't called, so I called her at 10:45 P.M. She said there were straggler customers and she had to stay a bit late, but she thought she had a ride. Then I heard nothing. I called her cellphone at 11:15 P.M. and got her recorded message. I called again, and again. I was really starting to worry because this had never happened before. I drove to the restaurant, but it seemed closed with no cars parked in front. It was now after 11:30 P.M., and Ben and I were starting to pace. We thought she might have made a mistake and accepted a ride from a customer. You know those awful thoughts about what can happen to your daughter! We were thinking the worst and were absolutely terrified. I realized I should have asked her who was giving her a ride. (She usually got a ride with a co-worker.) Finally, after an eternity, she showed up at 12:30 A.M. (on a weeknight!), just when I was ready to call the police in desperation.

"She acted completely surprised that we were, one, still up; and two, totally upset. Ben started the 'angry-dad thing,' so I told her he was angry because he was scared. I told her 'thank god' she was safe, and that we were upset because we didn't know if she was safe. It turned out that an ex-boyfriend had turned up at the restaurant, and they and a few of the other employees stayed for a while after closing. (I should have gone to the door when I drove by.) Kathy hadn't thought to call because (get this!) she hadn't actually gone somewhere else. She completely lost track of time and then her phone battery had died. So she apologized, and we forgave her, and the next morning we found this message on the dry-erase board:

Dear Parental Units:
I'm sorry I acted irresponsibly. My teenager self took over my usually responsible self. It won't happen again, I promise.
(She drew two images of herself—one as responsible and the other as her teenage self.)

To which I answered in red:

Dear Sweetie: It's okay. It's not easy being a teenager, but just know there are two people in this world that love you more than life itself, which is actually not always easy to take, but believe us it's a good thing."

As the mother of four, Helen has heard all the arguments. "We don't have a curfew as such," she explains, "but a system based on common sense and democratic negotiation. We discuss the activity, where he'll be going and with whom, and negotiate a time to be home that is appropriate for the activity. However, as the parent of underage children, I hold a non-negotiable veto in the event that one of them has lost all sense of judgement, which does happen. We stress that this is not about one's age, but a courtesy to the rest of the household. We grant more independence, depending on their behaviour. If they are self-motivated and willing to participate in the chores and responsibilities of home and school, this tells us they are becoming more aware of themselves and how they are connected to others. I've told my kids they would be very upset if I said I would be home at a certain time, and then didn't show up because I decided to amble around and do whatever I felt like, just because I'm old enough. It's not considerate."

I was guilty one night of the inconsiderate behaviour Helen describes, and inadvertently taught my teenage daughter what it is like to be on the receiving end. I was out with friends and my husband was out of town, so both daughters were home alone. I had told them I wouldn't be late, but the time flew by. Once I realized the lateness of the hour, I decided not to call home because I was certain they would be asleep and didn't want to waken them. (Doesn't this sound like a familiar teen excuse?) When I arrived home in the wee hours the older daughter was still up waiting for me, distraught with worry that something terrible had happened. Her first question was, "Why didn't you call me?" I apologized profusely, but inadequately. It was a memorable evening—for both of us. Recalling my poor daughter's emotional state, I can't in good conscience recommend that you engineer a similar event as a teaching strategy. But it was a powerful lesson for her about how painful it is to wait up for someone you love, and worry about why they aren't home yet. She never did this to me, and I never did it again.

So when it came to curfews for our daughters, I used my negligent behaviour as a model of what not to do, and kept the focus on communication. "Keep in touch. Do what I didn't do that fateful night—let us know where you are." Because my daughters knew that I was never deeply asleep until they were home safely, they tried to ease my mind by keeping me informed of their whereabouts. But I always emphasized that they should put their safety above all else—including making a curfew. I wanted to make certain that if they were debating whether it was worse to get into a car with a drunk, or get home late, they would miss their curfew and rouse me from my bed and explain the problem. And one of the beauties of text messaging is that you don't have to worry about your phone call waking up a sleeping household.

When it comes to setting curfew times, there is good reason for keeping a short leash when the teens are younger. One young man, just recently out of his teenage years, put the strategy succinctly. "Parents should set rules that are strict enough that they can be broken a bit without dire consequences." Debbie kept a good hold on her two boys in their pre-teen and early teen years. "It doesn't matter what you let your kids do, they'll immediately want to do more!" she said. "We set curfews that were tied to age— 11:00 P.M. at thirteen years, 11:30 P.M. at fourteen years, midnight at fifteen. And they were to come up to our bedroom to tell us they were home, whether we were asleep or not. When they were even younger we used to say, if you want freedom to do things away from us, just let us know where you are at all times, so we'll relax and give you that freedom. Back then they used to call us every time they changed houses! That same principle—the relationship between knowing where they were and freedom—carried on into the teenage years."

Jane negotiates curfews with her sixteen-year-old son to get him to practise using his own judgement. "When David lives at his dad's, his father sets the curfew," she explains. "David is expected to abide by it or there will be consequences. When David lives with me, I expect us to arrive at an agreed-upon curfew together. He'll say, 'What's my curfew?' and I respond, 'It all depends. It depends on whether it's a school night, who you're out with, where you're going, things like that.' So we work it out on a case-by-case basis. David is uncomfortable with my approach—but I'm holding my ground. It's always harder to be responsible for yourself than simply following someone else's rules—but I want him to start learning now." Jane decided to show David this explanation of how she saw the curfew issue and asked for his feedback. "He looked quite cross when he read it and said that I came across as extremely manipulative and controlling. He said it was 'controlling' for me to say curfew depends on the situation because presumably it could be arbitrary. When I asked whether giving him input into decisions that affect him is controlling he quickly backed away, saying he doesn't want to change how we work things out, he was just giving me a first impression. When I asked him if he would be more comfortable with one rule that would apply in all cases, he said this wouldn't be good. He's doing his job as a teenager and trying to figure things out."

The Parenting Teens website (see p. 266 for the URL) recommends taking the time to think the issues through in advance, and then establishing the rules with your teen's input. "Compromising when the curfew rules are being set and staying firm after the curfew has been agreed upon will lead to curfews that work for the whole family." The website compares the benefits of a blanket curfew (clear limits and boundaries) versus a curfew based on activities (time-consuming, but workable). They recommend setting a blanket curfew on the understanding that you can always modify it if your teen has something special to do or you need him to be home earlier. You can hear the voice of experience in this next tip. "Do not allow them to call half an hour before they are to be in to ask if they can sleep over at a friends. This is generally a red flag saying 'something is up.'"[6]

Sophia says her main memory of parenting teens was being frequently told she was the *only* parent who imposed a midnight curfew. When her daughters complained that no one else had to be home so early, her solution was to hold lots of events at her house.

Cars vs. Vehicles for Irresponsibility

Cars and teenagers can be a deadly combination and cellphones have aggravated the problem. A Pew Research Center study found that 52 percent of teenagers aged sixteen to seventeen who own a cellphone have talked on it while driving, about one-third have texted and 40 percent of teens say they have been in a car when the driver used a cellphone in a way that endangered them.[7] One approach to dealing with teens and driving is to ask them to sign a Safe Driving Contract such as the one developed by the I Promise Program, a collaboration of youth, parents and community members. The contract is an agreement between parent and youth whereby both parties agree to abide by safe-driving practices. The program provides a draft contract on their website (see p. 266 for the URL)[8] and recommends that parents and teens develop their own conditions through a process of discussion and negotiation. Topics in the sample contract include restrictions around cellphone use, driving sober and drug-free, hazardous conditions that may affect driving, limits on the number of passengers and awareness of physical issues, such as driving while tired, angry, upset, late or sick.

You can tell that teens were involved in developing the contract. One of the suggested commitments for the parent to make is "to trust my son/daughter and help him/her through difficult situations in as calm and non-judgemental a manner as possible." The contract also includes step-by-step instructions about what to do in the event of an accident, as well as a Collision Report Form to be kept in the glove compartment. The program's website is a storehouse of resources about teens and driving, including links to online videos about teen drivers on subjects such as "Prom & Drinking," "In Case of Crash" and "Operation Lifesaver," about safe driving near railway tracks.

To impress upon our teens the terrible consequences of mistakes made behind the wheel we could send them a link to the YouTube video produced by the Transport Accident Commission of the Australian government.[9] The video is a montage of commercials made for their road-safety campaigns, edited to the moving song "Everybody Hurts" by R.E.M. It is a powerful reminder of the way lives can be destroyed by unsafe driving. The emotional comments left on the website by viewers are a testament to the impact of the video.

Jane remembers that, of all the things that confronted her son Ryan as a teenager, automobiles were what scared her the most. "Small-town kids tend to get into car accidents more often than city teenagers. Speeding down country roads at night. Playing chicken. Just like they did in the movie *Rebel Without a Cause.* Ryan's friends all had expensive cars the minute they got their licences. They also had expensive ski equipment and ski passes to the mountain resorts, which were about a three-hour drive from home. You knew they would be tired at the end of a long ski day, likely having left at 5 A.M., and returning at 8 P.M. in heavy traffic. At least two of Ryan's friends were involved in Sunday-night accidents when they hit black ice while driving home from skiing. Several of them were involved in other kinds of car accidents as well, perhaps having to do with alcohol and driving, but more often it was just that they were inexperienced young men who had just learned to drive. I held my breath every Sunday night until Ryan got home from skiing, and was not unhappy to see winter end every year. I was thrilled when Ryan took up fly-fishing."

And what should your child do if he senses he will be a passenger with a reckless driver? We were very explicit about this situation. "Any time you are uncomfortable about getting into a car with someone—don't. Make an excuse and then call us." We would pick them up when they were younger. When they were older this was too humiliating, so we became very generous with taxi money—and we still consider it money well spent. Also, knowing they could get home safely on their own meant that we didn't have to interrupt our evening out—or be awakened from bed!

Emily had the same approach. "We have always emphasized that we would provide a ride and/or taxi money to our children or any of their friends. We need to renew these conversations with our younger son now, because he is just entering the age where he and his friends will be licenced drivers. I worry about teen drivers—trusting that whether they are the driver or the passenger, my sons will know when and how to say 'no' to a dangerous driving situation."

Jane remembers those late nights when it's hard to keep your part of the pact. "Ryan would never step into the car of another drunken teen. Even at 2 A.M., he knew he could call me and ask for a ride. It's easy to make a rule like this, but much harder to carry it out—at least for the parent. I remember vividly just how tough it could be, especially if I was tired and my precious teenager was at a party on the other side of town."

While the digital world is adding to the challenges our teens face around driving safely, activities are underway to turn the tables by developing digital devices to support good driving, and parents have been in the forefront. An iPhone app called *Slow Down* was commissioned by OVK, a Belgian organization for parents of children killed in road accidents. It uses our teen's own music to temper his inclination to speed. With a car full of friends and his favourite song playing full blast, it can be tempting to put the pedal to the metal to keep pace with the music. *Slow Down* uses GPS to work out his speed, compares it with the speed limit and, if he's going too fast, slows down the tempo of his music. If he breaks the limit by more than ten kilometres per hour (six miles per hour), then the music stops until he resumes the speed limit. Then there's *NOTXT n' Drive*, a BlackBerry app, also developed by the parent of a teen, that uses GPS to automatically restrict texting once a car reaches ten miles per hour.

House Party vs. Free-for-All

Parties were a bone of contention between teens and parents in our day, but now tools of the digital world, including cellphones, text messaging and MSN, allow house parties to get out of hand very quickly. A few invited guests can snowball into dozens and even hundreds, as word of the party spreads. Ginny remembers this happening a few years ago when she turned fourteen. "I invited twenty people to come to my house for my birthday party," she says, "and sixty people showed up—all invited through cellphones. It really scared me—and my parents!"

Parents have different tolerance levels for teen parties, but we need to agree on one thing: if your teenager is having a party, you must be present. And, as Debbie explains, being upstairs in bed may not be *present* enough. "My husband was away for Terry's eighteenth birthday," she recalls, "and Terry told me he was having a few friends over. I got into bed to read, thinking that it was enough to be home. Within an hour, the level of noise told me that this was *some* party, and I'd better be present. So I got up, got dressed and went downstairs. I plunked myself in the family room, which is open to the rest of the house, and pretended to be watching TV. I think Terry wasn't particularly happy to see me ('It's *alright*, Mum') but his friends didn't seem to mind. Two boys were drinking vodka straight. I went to each one and said, 'Sorry, that has to go away, no straight drinking in this house.' Both, though very drunk, and twice my size, put their bottles right away, and I kept my eye on them. What I learned from this experience was that my presence right in their midst was absolutely correct and absolutely necessary even if they were eighteen years old, and the kids really didn't mind. I think my son could have done without me but that's too bad, and there were no hard feelings in the end."

Because of problems Maria herself had experienced when she was eighteen years old, she was reluctant to allow her teenagers to have large house parties. "I learned first-hand how quickly situations can get out of control, even in your own home, when you combine alcohol with an influx of strangers," she explains. "My daughter finally understood my fears when she had a party in grade 11. I set a limit on numbers, prohibited alcohol, and then stayed in my room until the established departure hour, after which I came down to say good night. A couple of hours later (about 3 A.M.), I realized that not everyone had left, and I went down to investigate. Three young men were hiding—one in the storeroom, one in the laundry room and one behind the couch. These boys were older than my daughter, and I didn't know them. I very firmly, but politely, told them to go home, and they sheepishly came out of their hiding places and left. Earlier my daughter had asked them to leave, but they had refused to go, and she didn't know what to do. Because I was home, and paying attention, nothing bad happened. But that was the last time she asked to hold a party of that size."

And sometimes Maria just said "no" to parties, or came up with a compromise. "My older daughter often asked if she could have a house party, but we could never agree on limits on numbers of people or alcohol, so it just didn't happen. My youngest son asked to have an after-grad party for his whole graduating class plus girlfriends. We refused, but offered instead to have a dinner for twenty-five guests, and he was happy with the compromise. It's not fair for your teenager to have to take on the responsibility for everyone behaving themselves. And that memory of my teenage party gone bad will stay with me forever."

Janet tells the story of how she tried to keep parties under control by seizing cellphones. "When Meredith was eighteen she was the social convener of her gang, and the parties always seemed to be at our house. Everyone says that young people of this age shouldn't smoke or drink, but the reality is that they do. So the only question is where will they do it. I couldn't stand the thought of not knowing where Meredith was, and the chances of her being unsafe, so I preferred to put up with the ordeal of being the party house. I was always at home for the parties and so was my husband, if he was in town. We had one of my older sons or another strong young man around who was prepared to provide the muscle if things got out of hand. During this period we got to know the police quite well. It wasn't the kids in the house that were the problem—it was the ones on the street who caused the ruckus. Sometimes the kids hanging around outside were our guests out having a smoke; other times they were uninvited guests hoping to join the party. If things were noisy after midnight, the neighbours called the police. The police were actually very sympathetic and supported our attempt to provide a safe party place. But they told us to enforce two rules—for our own protection as much as for any one else's. During the party the guests should stay indoors, and after the party all the guests should go home in taxis. But I was getting fed up with the situation and found the whole thing lacking in basic consideration. So I came up with a rule that I felt would help keep the parties under control. I asked everyone to turn over their cellphone to me when they came in the door. In this way they couldn't call their friends and spread the word about where they were."

These stories illustrate a range of responses to hosting parties for teenagers in your own home, but you need to be aware of your legal responsibilities. It is also important to recognize the medical problems associated with teenage alcohol use, including the increased danger of alcohol dependency the earlier drinking starts. (See "Drinking vs. Alcoholism" on p. 188 for more discussion.)

If your teenager is at a party that seems to be spiralling out of control, he needs to know what to do. Running through some basic "what-if" scenarios with him, including a refresher in basic first aid, can be invaluable. Our daughter was at a party where a young man was being force-fed liquor straight from the bottle by his "friends." She probably saved his life when she recognized the symptoms of severe alcohol poisoning, and was quick-witted enough to call 911. She kept him conscious until the ambulance arrived, whereupon the attendants hooked him up to an intravenous tube and rushed him to the hospital. She found out later that when he got to emergency his blood alcohol level was so high they contemplated pumping his stomach. While all this was happening, the mother of the teenage host was apparently asleep upstairs.

It's also important for your teen to have a party exit strategy. My daughters remember me having a rule that they could call home anytime they were uncomfortable, and I would come and get them—no questions asked. My thinking was that if they had a choice between staying in an unsafe situation or facing parental wrath, I needed to emphasize that contacting us was the less scary option. They rarely took advantage of this policy, but I do recall occasionally getting out of bed and going to pick them up late at night—or at least after *my* bedtime. I remember one time thinking I'd gone too far with this policy. A group of parents had organized a taxi to bring our children home from a dance. For some reason, when the young people arrived to get into the car, the driver was extremely rude to them. My daughter and her friends told him, "We don't have to drive with you!" They refused to get into the car, and woke me up instead so that I would come and get them.

As I rubbed my sleepy eyes I remember thinking that maybe I had overdone the emphasis on politeness. But, of course, I'm glad they feel people should treat one another with respect, no matter what their age.

To make it easier for teenagers to extract themselves from difficult situations, some families develop a code. This allows their teen to signal that he wants to escape a situation, but saves him from embarrassing himself in front of his friends. For example, in one family their son will phone home and say something like "So is my hockey practice really at 6 A.M.?" meaning "Please come and pick me up."

There are a number of online resources designed to help teens party safely. Virtual Party (see p. 267 for the URL), a project of the Centre for Addiction and Mental Health (CAMH), was written by a group of young people. The website includes an interactive virtual party where you role-play as one of four characters, and make decisions about drinking, drugs and sex with a variety of consequences. The goal is to provide youth with information about alcohol, drugs and mental health issues, while emphasizing healthy choices and the reduction of harm. The site includes a resources page with links to organizations promoting teen health and safety.

The website www.safegrad.com (see p. 267) was set up by a local committee of students and professionals to address their concerns about teen parties, particularly proms and graduations. Problems around these events included alcohol use, impaired driving, increased drug use, poor sexual choices, vandalism and violence. The goal of the website is to help young people plan safe parties, and although some information is relevant only to the community of London, Ontario, the majority of the site is of general relevance, including a section on tips for parents holding parties at home.

The Grad Trip vs. Following the Pack

For many parents, the grad trip, organized by students to celebrate their graduation from high school, symbolizes the sense of entitlement that seems to be permeating teen life today. "Our eighteen-year-old son Colin assumed that we would bankroll his trip to Mexico," Debbie says. "My husband and I both feel strongly that these grad trips are fraught with danger. And we think there is something wrong with kids of that age seeing a week-long expensive drunk as their *entitlement*. Has our society gone crazy or what? So we said no and dug in our heels. It wasn't easy. There were hours of discussion and arguing, but we didn't budge. Colin's line was, 'I'm going to remember you deprived me of this for the rest of my life.' What we did do was offer to pay for the school history trip to Italy and Greece. We also said that if he wanted to get some friends together for a ski weekend in a nearby resort we'd pay half of the cost. And then the most amazing thing happened. Friend after friend dropped the grad-trip idea, and opted for the ski weekend and the school trip. One of the mothers rented a place on the ski hill, which they all shared while she lurked somewhere in the village with other friends (they won't rent to kids). And the school trip was fantastic. Our son was totally blown away by what he saw in Europe and saw only too well the difference between that and a one-week tear, and thanked us profusely. The one friend who did go to Mexico fell in the shower and woke up in a hospital having shards of glass taken out of his back!"

But Debbie's battles weren't over. "When it was time for our younger son to go on his grad trip, the arguing was even worse. Terry could not accept the fact that we would deprive him of what he considered would be the highlight of his life. His brother, knowing a good spectator sport when he saw one, intentionally added oil to the fire. Colin said that just because he hadn't been allowed didn't mean we shouldn't give in to number-two son. In Terry's case, we knew most of the parents of his best friends quite well. Terry was clearly the group leader, and we just dug in again and said no. Again, one by one, his friends opted to miss the grad trip and do the Italy/ski-weekend thing, and the parents all expressed their appreciation for our having taken a stand. I think that's the lesson here. When kids say 'everyone's doing it' and 'none of the other parents mind,' it's just not true. The same battles are going on in other homes and it only takes one to quickly change the flow. The big issue here is that parents are afraid to say no."

Lisa used the grad trip as an opportunity to teach her daughter that actions, or lack of them, had consequences.

"My efforts to help my son and daughter become responsible human beings involved household and school responsibilities for which they were held accountable through privileges and allowances tied in part to how they fulfilled those responsibilities. Hoping to have set the stage to avoid the sense of entitlement I saw in some of their affluent (or not) peers, I thought I would be the parent who cheered her teens on through their high-school and university years. Instead they were inconsistent students who only sometimes lived up to their potential and responsibilities, and I had to become the parent I didn't want to be. Consequences replaced privileges. When my daughter's barely passing marks arrived after I had paid the deposit for her grad trip, I cancelled her trip."

Your Teen's Issues vs. Your Own Issues

A difficult line to walk as we parent our teens is figuring out which issues are theirs and which are ours. When it comes to issues with the digital world, we may be projecting our own fears onto our children. Other times we are revisiting our own childhood struggles. In her book *Odd Girl Out*, Rachel Simmons describes a mother who inadvertently encouraged her daughter's relationship with a group of bullies because she was still fighting her own demons. The mother had grown up as an overweight child with few friends and had been on the receiving end of girls' meanness. Having a child brought out her old fears and insecurities, and she didn't want her daughter to know that pain. Determined that her daughter would be popular, she says, "I pushed her towards these people [the bullies]."[10]

Rachel's story emphasizes the need to remember that we are not our children. My daughter said this clearly one day when she was not much more than a toddler. I was urging her to wear more clothing because it was cold outside and she said, "My feelings are not the same as yours." Although she was saying that her metabolism ran at a different rate so that she didn't experience the cold in the same way, this truth applies to every aspect of her appreciation of the world. I've tried to remember her lesson.

Hannah explains how her father dealt with his own issues around horseback riding so that they wouldn't interfere with her enjoyment of the sport. "I loved animals and my entire family was allergic to everything, so I could only have animals that didn't live at home. So I had a horse, and I began to jump. My dad had been the doctor on call for the rodeo, and he had patched up people who had been thrown into fences and stomped on, and he was really, really nervous for me. So when I would go to these competitions he couldn't bear to be there. First, he thought he would bring me bad luck and, second, he didn't want to be the one to pick me up. So, because he and my mom were both too scared for me, I would go off to these things all by myself. They wanted me to do it—they just couldn't be there. When I finally did the Three-Day Event and I showed them around afterwards, all they could say was that they were so glad that they had no idea what I was doing because they were big jumps!"

Another tough job is to keep our ego under control when our children make decisions that are different from the ones we would have made. Author Barbara Kingsolver lays bare the roots of this issue in her "Letter to a Daughter at Thirteen." "People say it's because parents *love* their kids so much that they want to tell them how to live. But I'm afraid that's only half love, and the other half selfishness. Kids who turn out like their parents kind of validate their world. That was my first real lesson as a mother—realizing that you could be different from me, and it wouldn't make me less of a person."[11]

When my daughters' choices made me look bad among my peer group, I tried to remember that this was my problem not theirs. This happened most often when it came to issues around personal appearance. When I walked arm-in-arm with my bizarrely dressed daughters I would smile back at the adults who shot me disparaging looks. But I still felt the sting of their criticism. My daughter's blue hair was the subject of a parent-committee meeting at her conservative school, and some parents questioned my parenting skills, if not my sanity.

But it is when our teens' decisions are truly bad that we face the greatest challenges. "Despite your best efforts, things will go off the rails, and you'll find your ego is taking a beating," Helen says. "Your child might be caught stealing, doing drugs, engaging in early sexual experimentation.

When the story comes out, they need to hear that you have not lost faith in them, that everyone makes mistakes, that nothing is irredeemable. And this is when you, as the parent, really need to get a grip. You've heard adults express the sentiments. 'After all I've done for you!' 'And to think I would live to see the day when a child of mine . . . !' Stifle the urge. Work with them to move forward with the message 'I have faith in you, and we're going to get through this together.'"

Then there are the times when our own guilty feelings lead us to weigh in too heavily in our teen's battles. My mother remembers this happening to her when I moved to a new school. I was trying to break into a clique and was initially snubbed by Ellen. Although Ellen eventually became my best friend and we maintained our friendship for many years, my mother was never able to get over her dislike for her. At first my mother attributed her animosity to the fact that Ellen had made me so unhappy those many years ago—but she eventually acknowledged that the problem really lay in her own feelings of guilt around the fact that they had moved me, yet again, to another new school.

Self-awareness makes it easier to separate our issues from our teens and helps us parent more consciously. Emily used the memories of her own teenage years to understand and accept the behaviour of her sons. "I was a sullen, unhappy teen, mildly rebellious and totally unaware of how seriously my parents, especially my mother, took my negativity and criticism to heart. This knowledge helps me understand similar behaviour from my teens when it comes my way. Based on the way I was with my parents, I know the future holds better behaviour from them, and a much closer relationship with us. At the same time, I'm more likely than my mother to let them know how a particular remark or behaviour has hurt me."

Gloria used the memories of her own childhood to raise her son in a very different way. "My mother was very controlling and judgemental so that made it hard to feel her love. Sometimes I have an instinctive reaction to something my son says or does that comes straight from my mother in me. I work to put it aside to choose my own reaction, which I believe is far less judgemental, and leads to a better and closer relationship with my son. I feel I am charting new paths and am surprised at how I am unable to get shocked about some of the things my son does that would have shocked my mum. This poses challenges since my mother is continually questioning me about what my son is doing, and her advice is in the same mode she used to raise me."

Remembering that it's not about us helps us avoid taking things personally. "Some days, depending on their mood, teens would rather die than be seen walking side by side with a parental unit." Helen says. "They want to physically separate themselves from you. So, when they don't want to be warm and fuzzy in public, don't take it personally. This started with my boys when they were nine, and intensified up until about age sixteen. They wanted to show the world they were 'parent-free,' even if we were just ten feet behind them, following every move."

Ultimately we need to remember that our teenagers are on their own paths and we are becoming less important to the journey. "While teens are notoriously self-centred," Emily says, "I think it's just as hard for parents to realize that the quest for independence is explicitly not about them. When I think back to my late teens when I was (slowly) getting more mature and truly independent, I remember making lots of decisions that didn't involve my parents. That was an important line to cross, when I no longer did things designed to engage or infuriate my parents, but did them for my own reasons. I find it very hard now, as a parent, to remember that my sons' behaviour and decisions do not all use me as a reference point. And that they may not be excluding me or withholding information, and that if I ask them, they will share and sometimes even discuss things with me. But they are the decision makers and the consequence bearers for their own lives. It's hard not to feel 'left out' or even unappreciated but, at the end of the day, I get such pleasure out of seeing my sons acting in a way that is truly their own, and knowing that even if I can trace the roots of it back to our parenting efforts, the real credit belongs to my sons who put it together for themselves."

Learning vs. Teaching

We spend so much time focused on teaching our children, it's easy to miss the extraordinary opportunities we are given to learn from them. When I asked seventeen-year-old Stephanie about her advice to parents, she felt we would be less anxious about cyberspace if we understood it better. She recommends we take the opportunity to learn about the digital world from our teenagers. That way they get to be the teachers and we get to learn from them. Judging by the way older adults are flooding onto social-networking sites such as Facebook, we seem to be taking her advice. Forty-two percent of Internet users aged fifty and over now use social networking, with usage nearly doubling from 2009 to 2010.[12] And teenagers are probably responsible for some of our embrace of video conferencing, with more than half of Canadians reporting they use a webcam to stay in touch with loved ones.[13]

When Joan's daughter Megan gets a chance to share her computer skills with her parents, it gives her a real boost. "It's not often that our teens have an opportunity to teach their parents something," Joan explains. "Megan is not into competitive sports, and while she loves music, dance and drama, she is not particularly gifted at them. But she has had a computer from an early age and has a great aptitude for technology. She really enjoyed teaching her father how to operate his iPhone and showing him how to download apps onto his new toy. It's a good feeling for Megan and a get way for us to connect with her."

I find learning from my daughters to be one of the great joys of parenting. They get to experience the pleasure of imparting knowledge, and I get to live Michelangelo's philosophy of *ancora imparo* (I am still learning), attributed to him in his eighty-seventh year. When my daughter was a teenager she and her friends developed a tradition on

Mother's Day of taking their mothers to Latin dance clubs to teach us some moves. Seeing what good dancers our daughters were, we quickly realized just how frequently they visited these clubs! I continue to learn an appreciation for all things Latino from my daughter's love of their music, food, dance and languages. And I owe my knowledge of the Pharaohs to my daughter who doggedly pursued her dream of exploring the Nile, and dragged me along on her adventure. She was my guide as we explored the ruins and temples that she'd avidly studied.

Creativity is one of the great lessons we can learn from today's teenagers. When I watch our young people incorporate original thinking, art, singing and dancing into everyday life, I find it hard to buy the claims that multitasking has diminished creativity. Debbie, a former teacher, gives some credit to the current education system, and she makes sure to point out these improvements to her sons. "There is much less rote work, and much more emphasis on developing innovative approaches and really getting kids to think. I think they are enormously more imaginative than we were. I'd always comment on how lively and fun and innovative they and their friends were—whether it was the school assembly, or the yearbook or plans for a surprise party. I showed the boys my high-school yearbooks and we had a good laugh. Everyone sitting primly in rows, in uniform, and every picture being pretty much identical, whether it was the volleyball team, the class picture or the school choir. Their books, by contrast, were zany, graphic, funny and full of personality."

My daughters spent their teen years participating in the arts, both as performers and teachers, and they impress me with their creative approaches to problem solving, and the lateral thinking they employ to come up with innovative solutions. We'd be wise to pick up some of this creativity from our young people; developmental psychologist Howard Gardner identifies "the creating mind" as one of the five minds (capacities or perspectives) that people will need to thrive in the future. "Because almost anything that can be formulated as rules will be done well by computers," he say, "rewards will go to creators—those who have constructed a box but can think outside it."[14] And, as Richard Florida argues in his book *The Rise of the Creative Class*, creativity will be the decisive source of competitive advantage—both for nations and for individuals.

We all get to have more fun when this youthful creativity is reflected in mainstream culture—as we see in the make over of the 1978 musical *Grease*. Paramount Pictures is adding lyric subtitles to the film to produce a sing-along version that will appeal to young multi-taskers. They are hoping young people will come out in droves to dress up in costume and interact with the movie. As journalist Brooks Barnes sees it, "Sitting quietly in a theatre starts to feel like a bore when you can watch the DVD at home while texting a friend, playing a video game and posting witty comments on Facebook."[15]

We can learn from the bravado of teens. Many of them don't take themselves too seriously or let ego stand in the way of a good time. My daughter's friend is a two-hundred-pound star football and soccer player with enough nerve and sense of humour to enter a synchronized swimming competition. He and his similarly sized brother wowed the crowd with their antics and they won first prize. Most of us could do with a lot more play and risk-taking, and I hope our teenagers take these attributes with them into their adult lives.

Also, seeing the priority my daughters and their friends place on friendship has taught me an important life lesson. When my daughter's best friend experienced the unexpected death of her father, her friends dropped everything to surround her with love and support, twenty-four hours a day, for days on end. Looking back, her mother doubts they could have survived that period without that unwavering support. Examples of these acts of friendship are multiple among our circle of friends: a young man is injured in a skiing accident and his friend postpones university to help him rehabilitate; a young woman's sister is going through a bad patch so she changes schools to be closer to her and help her out; a young woman has a medical emergency and her friend comes from another city to stay with her through the procedures. We adults would do well to emulate these values.

Here's Catherine's story of loyalty and friendship, which takes place in a typical teenage setting. "Our son came home from a concert in a police car with two friends. They had purchased huge wine coolers and got quite drunk. The two other boys had lost the ability to function. They were incoherent, had lost all coordination and were vomiting.

Another concertgoer had punched one of them. Our son was not as drunk as his friends, and the police said he did not have to go home. However, he insisted on staying with his two very sick and drunk, and now bloodied, friends. He walked each of them into their homes and talked to their parents about why they were home so early, and then the police drove him home. He was embarrassed, ashamed and afraid that his friends' parents would not let him hang out with their kids any more. None of which happened. We made a point of telling him that we trusted him to never do that again. I believed he was really frightened by his experience of being out of control in a public place. I think that our reaction, which was to express fear for how close he came to really harming himself with both alcohol and other kids, was enough to scare him. I think if we had punished him more severely, it would have not been as effective. Did he learn something? I guess you could say that he stood by his friends and made sure they were all right—for which we were proud of him. On the other hand, he endangered himself."

Moving On vs. Getting Stuck

The transition from teen to independent adult seems to be difficult for many teens today. Having a life goal, or at least a plan for what to do after graduating from high school, can help our teen stick with school when he's bored and get him through the rough patches. But if you have a teenager who appears to be drifting, and your sage counsel seems to be falling on deaf ears, a message from a friend or relative may get through more effectively. In this regard, Gordon found that the relationship between his teenage son, Peter, and Peter's adult stepbrother had some real advantages. "George was fourteen years older than Peter, but still young enough to be cool," he says. "And Peter thought George's point of view had way more relevance to his life than mine. I saw this on a long road trip with my three boys to Oregon. We were going to my older brother's funeral, so the backdrop created some reference points for discussion. At the time Peter was fifteen years old, a competitive snowboarder, and not that keen on school. At one point George said, 'You know, Peter, when I was your age, I thought school was a waste of time. I wanted to be a professional mogul skier. But there were only two pros making a living at that time, and it didn't make much sense. Now you know there are quite a few professional snowboarders and the business is growing, so you could target that as a career. But you'll still need your grade 12.' That conversation had a big impact on Peter's attitude, and he started seriously thinking about university options. He also called George later to help him with some of his video-production assignments from school."

Once your teenager graduates from high school she may be at loose ends as to what to do next. Here's what Lisa did when both her son and daughter told her they didn't know what to do with their lives. "I told them they could stay at home, but they had to work and pay rent," she says. "They had been indifferent students in high school, so lest they squander the opportunity of a post-secondary education, I wanted them to contribute financially. We agreed that their rent would go towards their education if they went back to school, and it would go to me if they didn't. They both thought it was fair for me to ask them to invest in their education, and they thought the arrangement was fair. My son Grant immediately got a job selling skis and bikes, his passions at the time. I started to sense trouble when he said, 'It's not really like working, it's hanging out with friends.' Three years later, after annual one-hundred-dollar-a-month rent increases and no career or school plans, I gave him six months notice that unless he returned to school that September, he'd have to move out and see what life was really like on retail wages. True to form, Grant had no plans for either school or accommodation when September arrived, but he moved onto his friend's couch. He wasn't angry, and agreed it was the only way he'd learn the life lessons he needed. But I cried and felt sad it had to be that way. Four months later he was sharing a flat with a friend-of-a-friend and after a series of that type of arrangement, he moved to another city where his girlfriend was at university. Another series of couches and then finally he rented a flat for his girlfriend and himself, and returned to school full time while working at two jobs with the goal of being a kindergarten teacher—for which he's a natural."

Lisa's daughter Linda followed in her brother's footsteps. "Linda took longer to finish high school than necessary. Then, after much badgering and threatening from me, she got a coffee shop job that only lasted five months. She then chose not to apply for other jobs, even though they were readily available at the foot of our street. I badgered her some more to no avail, and then I gave her two months' notice that if she didn't pay rent, she'd have to move out. Without a job or money, this left her with two options. She could move in with her out-of-town father, or her jealous, controlling boyfriend, with whom she already spent most nights. It was far more difficult, painful, sad, and scary with my barely twenty-year-old daughter, than it had been with my twenty-two-year-old son. She chose the boyfriend. We helped her move her things—and we rarely heard from her for months. She asked to come for Christmas dinner, after which I saw her more frequently, but the boyfriend situation deteriorated. She was working but couldn't save enough for rent elsewhere. We rescued her after seven months when she begged to come home and promised to pay rent. Her return was sad-happy for me as I was so glad she was home and safe, but also so afraid of being hurt and disappointed by her again, and having to repeat the whole horrible scene again. Five months later, I realized my fears were unfounded: my daughter is perfect and we enjoy each other in ways that weren't possible for years. Although not back at school, she has a career goal, is working hard, and paying rent. She is a joy to be around and takes full responsibility for what she describes as her 'lost year.' She knows she has a deadline to either go back to school or move out to experience what life is really like on her wages."

Lisa looks back at these difficult years with her two children and concludes she did the right thing. "Would either of them have been where they are today had I let them continue to live at home? I'm sure not. Not only are they taking responsibility, moving forward and embracing the lives they've been given, they don't resent or blame me. I set clear expectations and held them accountable. I told them I loved them and couldn't facilitate their being stuck in dead-end/no jobs when they had the potential to contribute so much more to the world. Happy ending, yes; and perhaps best of all, I'm happier and closer to them than ever in a more-adult-than-parent relationship."

Even after your young adult officially leaves home, he may come back to live with you for periods of time. Opportunities like a summer job or a co-op placement may make him appreciate his parents' room and board. When June's son and daughter were both home for the summer after having been away all year she found she had to set new ground rules. She tried very hard to not comment on their lifestyle the way she might have when they were younger. But she did insist they keep in contact by phone so she wouldn't worry. She agreed to treat their rooms as their private space but, as the price of being back at home as a young adult, she insisted on tidy common areas. Under no condition was she going to pick up after them. She says her most significant stand came when her two children had a falling out that started to poison the atmosphere. June told them, "This home is a sanctuary for your dad and me, and we will not have our peace destroyed by your tensions. Fix this. Go to a counsellor, do whatever you need to do to work it out, but don't bring this problem home." June recalls, "They were quite taken aback by the forcefulness and clarity of my position, but they did work out their differences and peace was restored!"

Nancy Schaefer's book *Good Work! Get a Great Job or Be Your Own Boss: A Young Person's Guide* is full of useful advice to help your teen prepare for employment or starting their own business. The book was written in consultation with young job seekers and includes tips, checklists and question-and-answer advice from youth employment experts. Topics include building a résumé, writing cover letters, conducting yourself in interviews and networking to find opportunities. A section reviews what to do once you've landed the job and explains some basic elements of employment such as probation period, performance evaluation and payroll deductions.

Understanding the Teen vs. Being the Adult

It will help us parent our teen if we understand their world, but ultimately we must be the adult. "I always try to see things through the eyes of a thirteen-year-old or an eighteen-year-old," Catherine says, "then I act like a parent."

Reading Anne Frank's remarkable diary is an excellent way to see life through a teen's lens. From age thirteen to fifteen Anne kept a journal when she was in hiding with her family in Amsterdam during World War II. Although she was writing half a century ago in a horrifying and unique context, the fundamentals of adolescence she describes are timeless—the rollercoaster moods, problems getting along with her parents, the physical changes of puberty, and the longings and disappointments of first love. She documents her kaleidoscope of emotions with remarkable self-awareness—anger about family favouritism, disgust at adult behaviour and hypocrisy, sorrow at being misunderstood, anguish at being underestimated, dissatisfaction with herself and irritation at being continually on the receiving end of adult criticism and lectures. She wished her parents had opened themselves up to her during this time, so she could have "tread upon more intimate ground" with them and wanted them to treat her as an individual with unique problems, rather than someone suffering from "symptoms of your age."[16]

The writer Stephen J. Lyons got another perspective on what it feels like to be a teenager when he assigned a high-school class the writing topic "What are you afraid of?" His compilation of the responses is an illuminating catalogue of teenage angst: "Making a mistake. Rapists. Going to college. Becoming my father. Staying the same too long. The environment becoming bad. The future. Death of a loved one. Admitting my love for another. Spiders. My grandmother's perfume. Losing my convictions. Loneliness. Leaving behind what I love. Prejudice. Being torn from all I believe in. Not being able to make a difference. Machines. Dark basements. Raising my children wrong."[17]

Understanding the developmental tasks that teenagers face helped Carol take the high road and deal with her daughters' unpleasant behaviour with more maturity. "When I was feeling hurt, my friend would remind me that one of a teenager's main jobs is to gradually break away and move towards independence, and to break out of the nest requires a strong sharp beak. So when my daughters were being particularly hostile and angry, and could barely stand to be in the same room with me, I would remind myself that it was not strictly personal, and take some comfort in this."

Louann Brizendine, the neuropsychiatrist who wrote *The Female Brain*, puts it bluntly: "As a parent of teens, you have the job of ignoring much of what they say. Don't take any impulsive or emotional tirades seriously. Stay calm. Teens state their intentions—and feel them—with such passion that you can be persuaded in spite of yourself. Just remember, your teen daughter's impulse-control circuits can't handle the input. Like it or not, you must provide the control while her brain cannot."[18] As my daughter says, "There were times when I really wanted to be nice, or pleasant or kind—but I just couldn't." And we can remember from our own childhood the pain, from loneliness or fear, that a teen's insolent or uncaring attitude may be covering.

And we can be grateful that our teens trust us enough to be who they are—warts and all. Jean Vanier writes about this in his book *Becoming Human*, when describing the silence of abandoned orphans. "We cry out only when there is hope that someone may hear us."[19] One technique for coping is to tap into that powerful love you felt when your child was born—that unconditional love that says, "you are beautiful, it is so good you are alive." Dig deep to find that perfect baby who may now be camouflaged in a pretty rough and rude exterior.

One way of staying connected to your love during trying periods is to remember, "this too shall pass." Harold talks about going through a bad patch with his teenage daughter, and coming out happily on the other end. "My wife and I divorced when our son and daughter were young. My wife had custody of the children and for many years we lived in different cities. After we separated, I made a commitment that I would communicate in some way with both children every day. And I did. I called, wrote and faxed (this was pre-Internet!). The children also spent large chunks of time with me during holidays and in the summer. When my daughter was in her mid-teens I remember going through a very painful period. I felt I had lost the wonderful relationship I had built with her when she was younger, and I had no idea why. When my daughter turned twenty-two and we had found each other again, I asked her what had happened. I said to her, 'You know, when you were growing up I thought you went through a patch when you really didn't like me.' She replied, with wisdom beyond her years, 'It wasn't you I didn't like, Daddy, it was me.'"

Maria also remembers repeating the mantra "this too shall pass," but wondering when. While their four children were growing up, her family had to move several times to different cities. The two older teenagers reacted very badly to one move in particular and Maria remembers their anger subsiding only after a long period of estrangement. "Our most difficult move was when Laura was sixteen. She had a meltdown when we told her we were moving. She told her father that he was responsible for 'ruining her life,' and then she ran away from home. Michael, fifteen at the time, didn't take the news well either. He punched holes in the wall with his fist.

"We knew where Laura was, and we knew she was safe. Her best friend's parents were very understanding, and let Laura cool down for a few days in their home. It was just before Christmas and we told Laura that if she wanted her new cellphone she had to come home on Christmas Eve, and she had to behave herself. She did, but the silent treatment began the day after Christmas and basically she had as little to do with us as possible for a good year. We understood that Laura and Michael did have huge adjustments to make, and we tried to be as patient and accommodating as we could. It was hard, but we tried not to take anything too personally. Laura, in particular, could be very surly and uncommunicative, and we tried not to overreact. By the end of their first year much had improved. Today Laura acknowledges her thorny behaviour towards us during this difficult time. She cautioned her younger brother (who also had to make a major move with us when he was sixteen) not to react the way she had. His transition went smoothly, but then, he'd had advice from an old pro!"

Debbie reminds us that the stormy behaviour might only last a few hours before the sun returns. "When Colin was ten years old he called from his friend Jason's place to ask if he could go to the dance at our local community centre with Jason and Jason's twelve-year-old brother. These dances were generally for twelve- to fourteen-year-olds and ended about 10 P.M. I said 'no,' that I thought dances weren't for ten-year-olds. I was in bed reading and several minutes later Colin burst in the front door, slamming it with great drama and yelling 'For f***'s sake!' Jason had been allowed to go and why couldn't he, etcetera, etcetera. He roared and ranted for a while and then I heard silence, so I just kept on reading. Next thing I know, he's by my bedside in his pajamas, with freshly made popcorn, and he climbs in with me, happy as a clam. Then I knew for sure he'd never really wanted to go. He was just pushing me, and he was happy I'd pushed back."

When we're trying to be the parent, there are some behaviours that are unworthy of an adult. "These are certain things that I would never do to my teenagers—name calling, humiliation, withholding love, ridiculing their thoughts, ideas and emotions, physical violence, emotional manipulation," says Helen. "Move yourself forward to when you are in your eighties. Your child is now responsible for your welfare. How would you want to be treated? What you sow is what you reap." She tells the story of how she tried to model mature behaviour by owning up when she was wrong. "I accused my children of stealing some money, only to find the cash just where I had put it—in the pocket of a spare coat. I apologized profusely, causing great guffaws from the wrongly accused, but gaining some respect for the way I had eaten crow—with dignity."

Helen also begs us not to try to look and/or act like a teenager. "Many of we boomers seem to be trying to stop the aging process by adopting a youth culture—including their music, their language and their dress style. The more we invade their world, the more we force them into more marginal activity in order to find their own space. Stay square—it's annoying but comforting! And you'll give them a whole lot more space to rebel—safely!"

My friend, Rohini Ramanathan uses the beautiful image of parent as riverbank in her advice on how a parent should guide his/her young wards. "My recommendation, more as a parent myself and a critical thinker, is, we need to understand the pulse of the times and society we live in; be aware of the pressures our youngsters are subject to; be careful with our words and deeds towards them; balance experts' advice with our own God-given instincts, intelligence and experience and play the parental role the way the riverbank protects, directs and 'comforts' the river that flows alongside of it."[20]

I love this concept of parent as riverbank because it reminds us, as we guide our teenagers, that our steadfast strength needs to be tempered with a giving flexibility. When we hold our teenagers in a firm but loose embrace we can support the river through the spring floods that cause it to overspill its banks, we can adjust our shoreline to its daily moods, and we can give easement when it leaves its old channel and forges a fresh one. And, from time to time, we need to stop directing, containing and advising, and simply admire the miracle that is the river. We need to pause and feast on the beauty and the energy and the raw goodness that is our teenagers, for soon they'll be all grown up and we will never see that river water again.

Conclusion

AFTER READING all these stories and exploring the recommended books and websites, you'll have the resources you need to design strategies that are tailor-made for you and your teenager. And because you'll be more familiar with what lies ahead, you should become a more confident parent, and be more relaxed, and have more fun.

Most importantly, I don't want you to come away from this book feeling that the task of parenting a teen is overwhelming, and that you can't possibly live up to all the expectations. The wise Anne Frank reminds us that there is only so much we can do. "Parents can only give good advice or put [their children] on the right paths, but the final forming of a person's character lies in their own hands."[1]

As writer Fay Weldon explains, it is easier to relax about parenting if you have had more than one child. But her viewpoint applies to seasoned parents of singletons, too. "You've seen it all happen before, and they've somehow survived. They go through bad patches and good. They've stayed out late and they've come back, eventually. You know that whatever they may be like at one stage, they will change yet again. And that they will eventually return to the temperament they revealed in the first few weeks of their life, which is what seems to happen. That's why new babies are so interesting."[2]

But probably the most important thing to remember is that you are not raising your teenager alone. None of us is capable of being all things to our children, and chances are very good that if you can't provide something, your teen will find it elsewhere. I have seen this truth most clearly with our daughters when it came to the "domestic arts," for which I have no talent and even less interest. My husband has more culinary talent than I do, but he would rather be canoeing with them than providing cooking instruction. From time to time people would say to me, "How will your daughters ever learn to cook when you've never taught them a thing?" Fortunately, although I didn't inherit a domestic-goddess gene, I also didn't get a guilt gene, so I would reply with something like, "Oh, they'll figure it out when they need to." I am pleased to report that indeed it happened just like that. Both our daughters can feed themselves and one of them has turned into a superb cook, capable of single-handedly preparing a Thanksgiving dinner with all the trimmings. When I hired her to cater for a small dinner party, one of the guests said he would offer her a job in his company based on the logistical talents she had demonstrated, preparing a delicious and perfectly orchestrated four-course meal from scratch. Whom should we thank for transferring these skills? The TV food and cooking shows of Anthony Bourdain and Nigella Lawson, combined with www.marthastewart.com. As they say, when the student is ready the teacher will appear.

And if I haven't convinced you yet that you should be grateful for being a parent today, here is another reason, and it is the most profound: Parenting in these times gives us a front-row seat for a performance of extraordinary cultural change. As technology begins to permeate all aspects of our lives, we are partnered with our children in a dynamic dance that is reshaping our society, and we are making it up as we go along. At the same time as we are guiding our children through the implications of living a life online, we are working through many of the same issues for ourselves. We are asking ourselves questions about our own digital addiction, our own over-sharing in cyberspace and our own life balance in a world of constant connection. Continually engaging with our children as we confront these challenges heightens our understanding of the changes, helps us carve out our own solutions, and forces us to really pay attention. We are both audience and participant in the biggest event of our lives.

Websites for Parents

The following websites are discussed in the text and are presented in the order in which they appear in the text.

THE TEEN MIND

Practising for Life vs. Wasting Time

Center for Internet Addiction Recovery:
www.netaddiction.com

Educating vs. Monitoring

WiredSafety: www.wiredsafety.org
Media Awareness Network: www.media-awareness.ca
Wired Kids, Inc.: www.wiredkids.org
eBlaster: www.eblaster.com

Fun vs. Obsession

ParentFurther: www.parentfurther.com

Multi-tasking vs. Inability to Focus

www.mysummercamps.com
www.camps.ca
www.hathayogalesson.com

Staying the Course vs. Dropping Out

www.ourkids.net/school/
Learning Disabilities Association of America:
   www.ldanatl.org
Learning Disabilities Association of Ontario:
   www.ldao.ca

THE SOCIAL TEEN

Sexting vs. Criminal Behaviour

Reputation.com: www.reputation.com

Real Friends vs. Virtual Friends

WiredSafety: www.wiredsafety.org

Privacy vs. Anonymity

Wired Kids, Inc.: www.wiredkids.org

Sexual Well-being vs. Sexual Health

It's a Teen's World: www.itsateensworld.com
Justine Henning: www.readingpenpals.com
Planned Parenthood Toronto: www.spiderbytes.ca
Middlesex-London Health Unit: www.healthunit.com
www.kidshealth.org

THE TEEN SPIRIT

Self-esteem vs. Narcissism

The Narcissistic Personality Inventory:
   http://psychcentral.com/quizzes/narcissistic.htm

Empathy vs. Indifference

Youth Noise: www.youthnoise.com
Free The Children: www.freethechildren.com
Me to We: www.metowe.com

Depressed vs. Chemically Imbalanced

Mind Zone: www.copecaredeal.org
Check Up from the Neck Up:
   www.checkupfromtheneckup.ca
Mind Your Mind: www.mindyourmind.ca
www.mentalhealth4kids.ca
Laing House: www.lainghouse.org
Nova Scotia Early Psychosis Program:
   http://earlypsychosis.medicine.dal.ca

Sexual Identity vs. Sexual Confusion

www.kidshealth.org
Planned Parenthood Toronto: www.spiderbytes.ca
It Gets Better Project: www.youtube.com/itgetsbetter
project

Children's Mental Health Ontario

www.kidsmentalhealth.ca

THE TEEN CITIZEN

Financial Acumen vs. Spending Skills

The Canadian Bankers Association:
  www.yourmoney.cba.ca
Investor Education Fund:
  www.getsmarteraboutmoney.ca
Junior Achievement: www.ja.org

Intervening vs. Standing By

www.cyberbullying.org
www.bullying.org
www.stopbullyingnow.hrsa.gov/kids/
www.speerssociety.gov
National Youth Violence Prevention Resource Center:
  www.safeyouth.org
www.equalityrules.ca

Global vs. Insular

Food Force: www.food-force.com
People Power:
  http://www.aforcemorepowerful.org/game/index.php
Darfur Is Dying: www.darfurisdying.com
Peacemaker: www.peacemakergame.com
Ayiti: http://costoflife.ning.com
Transitions Abroad: www.transitionsabroad.com

THE TEEN BODY

Self-Acceptance vs. Self-Aversion

www.plasticassets.com
www.about-face.org
http://loveyourbody.nowfoundation.org
Adbusters Media Foundation: www.adbusters.org
KidsHealth: www.kidshealth.org
National Eating Disorders Association:
    www.nationaleatingdisorders.org
Beautiful Women Project:
    www.beautifulwomenproject.com

Body Decoration vs. Body Mutilation

www.kidshealth.org

Smokefree vs. Nicotine-Addicted

Foundation for a Smokefree America:
    www.anti-smoking.org
http://smokefree.gov

Drinking vs. Alcoholism

Center for Adolescent Substance Abuse Research at
Children's Hospital Boston: www.teen-safe.org
www.checkyourdrinking.net
www.factsontap.org

Getting High vs. Getting Hooked

Parent Action on Drugs: www.parentactionondrugs.org

Children Now:
  http://www.childrennow.org/index.php/learn/talking_with_kids/

www.theantidrug.com

National Institute on Drug Abuse (NIDA):
  www.teens.drugabuse.gov

U.S. Drug Enforcement Administration:
  www.justthinktwice.com

Eating vs. Controlling

National Eating Disorder Information Centre:
  www.nedic.ca

National Eating Disorders Association:
  www.nationaleatingdisorders.org

National Association of Anorexia Nervosa and Associated Disorders: www.anad.org

Sheena's Place: www.sheenasplace.org

THE TEEN-PARENT CONNECTION

Curfew vs. Power Struggle

Parenting Teens: http://parentingteens.about.com

Cars vs. Vehicles for Irresponsibility

I Promise Program: www.ipromiseprogram.com

House Party vs. Free-for-All

Centre for Addiction and Mental Health (CAMH)
Virtual Party: www.virtual-party.org
Safegrad.com: www.safegrad.com

Notes

BACKGROUND

1 Tyler Clementi, a Rutgers University freshman, jumped off the George Washington Bridge after his roommate and a female friend posted a videocam feed of Clementi's intimate encounter. Lisa W. Foderaro and Winnie Hu, "Before a Suicide, Hints in Online Musings," *New York Times*, 30 September 2010.

2 Helen Carter, "Facebook killer sentenced to life for teenager's murder," *Guardian*, 8 March 2010.

THE TEEN MIND

1 Victoria J. Rideout, Ulla G. Foehr and Donald F. Roberts, *Generation M²: Media in the Lives of 8- to 18-Year-Olds* (Washington: Kaiser Family Foundation, 2010).

2 A Pew survey on social media and mobile Internet use among teens and young adults reported that 93 percent of teens ages twelve to seventeen go online, as do 93 percent of young adults ages eighteen to twenty-nine. Seventy-three percent of wired teens use social-networking websites, 14 percent of online teens say they blog, and 8 percent of Internet users ages twelve to seventeen use Twitter. Amanda Lenhart, Kristen Purcell, Aaron Smith and Kathryn Zickuhr, *Social Media & Mobile Internet Use Among Teens and Young Adults*

(Washington: Pew Research Center, 2010). A Pew survey on teens and mobile phones reported that 75 percent of twelve- to seventeen-year-olds own cellphones and 88 percent of them are using text messaging. Teen girls aged fourteen to seventeen send more than 100 text messages per day. Amanda Lenhart, Rich Ling, Scott Campbell and Kristen Purcell, *Teens and Mobile Phones* (Washington: Pew Research Center, 2010).

3 Tara Parker Pope, "An Ugly Toll of Technology: Impatience and Forgetfulness," *New York Times*, 7 June 2010.

4 Amy Dempsey, "iPhone app pays off for boy genius," *Toronto Star*, 4 August 2010.

5 ERIN Research, *Young Canadians in a Wired World: Phase 11: Student Survey* (Ottawa: Media Awareness Network, 2005).

6 *Ibid.*, 8.

7 Brad Stone, "Now Parents Can Hire a Hall Monitor for the Web," *New York Times*, 4 July 2010.

8 Gordon Neufeld and Gabor Maté, *Hold On to Your Kids* (Toronto: Vintage Canada Edition, 2005), 73.

9 MSN refers to MSN Messenger, a form of instant messaging.

10 Amanda Lenhart, Joseph Kahne, Ellen Middaugh, Alexandra Macgill, Chris Evans and Jessica Vitak, *Teens, Video Games and Civics* (Washington: Pew Research Center, 2008).

11 Harris Interactive poll released in January 2008 as reported by the Media Awareness http://www.media-awareness.ca/english/parents/video_games/issues_teens_videogames.cfm.

12 These estimates are from a 2007 Harris poll reported in the *Globe and Mail*, 16 October 2010, and are probably low since the games have gained wider and more committed audiences since then.

13 For a complete description of the game, see http://en.wikipedia.org/wiki/World_of_Warcraft.

14 The article "How to Break a World of Warcraft Addiction" can be found at http://www.wikihow.com/Break-a-World-of-Warcraft-Addiction. (Accessed March 14, 2011.)

15 Lawrence T. Lam and Zi-Wen Peng, "Effect of Pathological Use of the Internet on Adolescent Mental Health," *Arch Pediatr Adolesc Med.*, published online 2 August 2010, doi:10.1001/archpediatrics. 2010. 159.

16 http://www.commonsensemedia.org/expert-interview-constance-steinkuehler.

17 Nicholas L. Carnagay, Craig A. Anderson and Brad J. Bushman, "The effect of video game violence on psychological desensitization to real-life violence," *Journal of Experimental Social Psychology*, 43 (2007) 489–496.

18 The *Checklist for Violent Youth* is available at the website of the Media Awareness Network http://www.media-awareness.ca/english/resources/tip_sheets/violent_youth.cfm (accessed 15 March 2011).

19 The "Guide to Video Game Addiction" can be downloaded from the ParentFurther website at http://www.parentfurther.com/technology-media/video-games/addiction (accessed 15 March 2011).

20 For a good description of the ROFL world see Rob Walker's article "When Funny Goes Viral" in the *New York Times Magazine*, 18 July 2010.

21 Nicholas Carr, *The Shallows: What the Internet Is Doing to Our Brains* (New York: W.W. Norton & Company, 2010), 10.

22 Yukari Iwatani Kane and Ian Sherr, "Apple iPhone 4 executive leaves company," *Globe and Mail*, 9 August 2010.

23 Ana Homayoun, *That Crumpled Paper Was Due Last Week* (New York: Perigee Book, 2010), 121.

24 John D. Sutter, "Trouble sleeping? Maybe it's your iPad," CNN, 13 May 2010 http://edition.cnn.com/2010/TECH/05/13/sleep.gadgets.ipad/index.html?hpt=C1.

25 Silken Laumann, *Child's Play* (Toronto: Random House Canada, 2006), 111.

26 *Ibid.*, 40.

27 See details at http://www.olympic.org/content/YOG.

28 Olivia Barker, "Can summer camps revive the lost art of letter writing?" *USA Today*, 27 July 2010.

29 Steven Johnson, "Yes, People Still Read, but Now It's Social," *New York Times*, 20 June 2010.

30 "A week without Facebook? U.S. college tries it out," *Globe and Mail*, 17 September 2010.

31 According to the Canadian Institute for Health Information (CIHI). See www.cihi.ca.

32 Matt Richtel, "Growing Up Digital, Wired for Distraction," *New York Times*, 21 November 2010.

33 In 2009–10, 191,000 (8.5 percent) of young people aged twenty to twenty-four had not completed a high-school diploma and were not attending school. Dropout rates were lower for young women (6.6 percent) than for young men (10.3 percent). See http://www.statcan.gc.ca/daily-quotidien/101103/dq101103a-eng.htm.

34 See "Early indicators of students at risk of dropping out of high school" at http://www.statcan.gc.ca/pub/81-004-x/2004006/7781-eng.htm#a.

35 "Failing Boys: Probing the Problem," in Our Time to Lead, *Globe and Mail*, 16 October 2010.

36 Carolyn Abraham, "From fun-focused to career-minded," *Globe and Mail*, 18 October 2010.

THE SOCIAL TEEN

1   See http://thetyee.ca/News/2007/04/23/Feldmar/.

2   "Five errors to avoid when using the Web," *Globe and Mail*, 9 October 2010.

3   You can see the photo at http://www.podcastingnews.com/2007/12/30/myspace-party-pic-cost-stacy-snyder-job/.

4   Andrew Levy, "Teenage office worker sacked for moaning on Facebook about her 'totally boring' job," *Daily Mail*, 26 February 2009.

5   Scott Rosenberg, *Say Everything* (New York: Crown Publishers, 2009), 35.

6   *Ibid.*, 42.

7   See http://www.parentfurther.com/teens-and-sexting.

8   Louann Brizendine, *The Female Brain* (New York: Morgan Road Books, 2006), 34.

9   Dakshana Bascaramurty, "Grandma's lap? Try her laptop," *Globe and Mail*, 26 July 2010.

10 As of December 29, 2010.

11 Jeffrey Rosen, "The Web Means the End of Forgetting," *New York Times*, 19 July 2010.

12 Quoted in "The Web Means the End of Forgetting" by Jeffrey Rosen, *New York Times*, 19 July 2010.

13 Rod Mickleburgh and Wendy Stueck, "After alleged gang-rape, teen's parent 'a ball of rage,'" *Globe and Mail*, 18 September 2010.

14 Madeline Levine, *The Price of Privilege* (New York: HarperCollins, 2006), 120.

15 *Young Canadians in a Wired World* Student Survey, for Media Awareness Network by ERIN Research, November 2005. See www.media-awareness.ca.

16 Quoted in Peggy Orenstein, "I Tweet, Therefore I Am," *New York Times*, 1 August 2010.

17 Rosenberg, *Say Everything*, 89.

18 Malcolm Gladwell, *Blink* (New York: Little, Brown and Company, 2005), 54.

19 Robert Fulford, *The Triumph of Narrative: Storytelling in the Age of Mass Culture* (Toronto: House of Anasi Press, 1999), 33.

20 Christy Haubegger, "An Idea of My Own" in *Girls Like Us* (Novato, California: New World Library, 1999), 181.

21 Amanda Lenhart, *Teens, Stranger Contact & Cyberbullying* (Washington: Pew Research Center, 2008).

22 Janis Wolak, et al., "Online 'Predators' and Their Victims: Myths, Realities, and Implications for Prevention and Treatment," *American Psychologist*, 63, no. 2, 111–28 (February–March 2008), available at http://www.annenbergonlinecommunities.com.

23 Professor Barry Wellman, the Director of NetLab at the University of Toronto, has done extensive research on this topic. See http://homes.chass.utoronto.ca/~wellman/publications/.

24 Eva Salinas, "Grades go up when students face the music," *Globe and Mail*, 5 May 2006.

25 Neufeld and Maté, *Hold On to Your Kids*, 103.

26 Piper talks about this in her foreword to *Girls Like Us*, edited by Gina Misiroglu, cited above.

27 Wilma Mankiller, "Child of the Sixties," in *Girls Like Us*, 167.

28 See the details at http://www.guardian.co.uk/books/2010/jul/16/orlando-figes-fake-amazon-reviews.

29 The video is at www.youtube.com/watch?v=IPe_hf7aBXM.

30 For more on information embedded in photos and videos see the website of the International Computer Science Institute at http://www.icsi.berkeley.edu/.

31 Robert Lemos, "Your Apps Could be Leaking Private Info," *MIT Technology Review*, 2 August 2010, http://www.technologyreview.com/computing/25921/?a=f.

32 Mary Madden and Aaron Smith, *Reputation Management and Social Media* (Washington: Pew Research Center, 2010).

33 Claire Cain Miller, "The Many Faces of You," *New York Times*, 17 October 2010.

34 Roni Caryn Rabin, "Behavior: Too Much Texting is Linked to Other Problems," *New York Times*, 9 November 2010.

35 *Ibid.*

36 Andrea Gordon, "Growing up with sex and tech," *Toronto Star*, 4 December 2010.

37 Naomi Wolfe, "Wild Things," *New York Times Book Review*, 12 March 2006.

38 Personal correspondence (e-mail): 23 May 2006.

39 Alicia Chang, "High school confidential: Teens' sex life can help schoolwork, study finds," *Globe and Mail*, 16 August 2010.

40 Sharon Hersh, *"Mom, Sex Is No Big Deal"* (Colorado Springs: Shaw Books, 2006), 6.

41 According to the Canadian Institute for Health Information (CIHI). See www.cihi.ca.

42 In this online survey of youth between thirteen and twenty-four years of age, drugs and substance abuse had the number two spot, with the balance of the issues in this descending order: unhealthy relationships (abuse), mental health and depression, alcohol abuse, body image and eating disorders. The ranking was fairly consistent across all age groups and ethnicities, with the exception of body image and eating disorders, which older respondents ranked successively higher. The ranking was also fairly consistent by gender. "Youth Mental Health and Wellness: Core Issues and Views on Existing Resources," 2008. See http://www.youthnoise.com/site/images/Youth_Mental_Health_and_Wellness.pdf.

43 See http://www.healthunit.com/article.aspx?ID=15160.

THE TEEN SPIRIT

1 Michael Ventura, "Screenworld: Reality isn't what it used to be," *Psychotherapy Networker*, http://www.psychotherapynetworker.org/recentissues/539-screenworld.

2 *Ibid.*

3 For a description of the new networked family as compared with the way family used to be, see *Networked: The New Social Operating System* by Lee Rainie and Barry Wellman (Cambridge, MA: MIT Press, 2012).

4 Levine, *The Price of Privilege*, 33.

5 Neufeld and Maté, *Hold On to Your Kids*, 103.

6 Nicki Thomas, "Police trauma dog comforts classmates of murdered teen," *Toronto Star*, 2 October 2010.

7 Matt Richtel, "Outdoors and Out of Reach, Studying the Brain," *New York Times*, 15 August 2010.

8 Hal Niedzviecki, *Hello, I'm Special* (Toronto: Penguin Canada, 2004), xvi.

9 Benedict Carey, "A Snapshot of a Generation May Come Out Blurry," *New York Times*, 2 August 2010.

10 Mara Sidoli, *The Unfolding Self: Separation and Individuation* (Boston: SIGO Press, 1989), 163.

11 *Ibid.*, 71.

12 Levine, *The Price of Privilege*, 29.

13 Jean Vanier, *Becoming Human* (Toronto: House of Anansi Press Ltd., 1998), 89.

14 See http://www.ns.umich.edu/htdocs/releases/story.php?id=7724.

15 See http://www.brightsurf.com/news/headlines/26193/Feelings_matter_less_to_teenagers.html.

16 *National Survey of Giving, Volunteering and Participating* (Toronto: Imagine Canada, 2002).

17 Craig Kielburger and Marc Kielburger, "'Apathetic Alex' found his voice in volunteering," *Toronto Star*, 27 April 2006.

18 Norah McClintock, *Understanding Canadian Volunteers* (Toronto: Canadian Centre for Philanthropy, 2004), 7.

19 According to an Ipsos Reid survey, 3 July 2009, parents whose children were performing at an above-average level in school and were

involved in their local communities nearly unanimously agree (97 percent) that the community involvement helped their children succeed both inside and outside the classroom. See http://www.ipsos-na.com/news/pressrelease.cfm?id=4450.

20 Leonard Davidman, To the Editor, *New York Times*, 21 November 2010.

21 "Youth who self-identify as gay, lesbian or bisexual at higher suicide risk," McGill Newsroom, 5 February 2010, http://www.mcgill.ca/newsroom/news/item/?item_id=114726.

22 Located at http://kidshealth.org/teen/sexual_health/guys/sexual_orientation.html (accessed 16 March 2011).

23 See http://www.thestranger.com/seattle/SavageLove?oid=4940874.

24 For an overview of the mountain of academic research on the show see http://www.slayage.tv.

25 From "The Field" by Persian poet Jalal Ad-Din Rumi (1207–1273).

THE TEEN CITIZEN

1 David Elkind, *The Hurried Child* (Cambridge, MA: Da Capo Press, 2007), 210.

2 Gladwell, *Blink*, 43.

3 Michael Osit, *Generation Text: Raising Well-Adjusted Kids in an Age of Instant Everything* (New York: AMACOM, 2008), 86.

4 *Ibid.*, 85.

5 Marian Wright Edelman in "A Family Legacy," *Girls Like Us*, 95.

6 Thomas Friedman, *The World Is Flat* (New York: Farrar, Straus and Giroux, 2005), 303.

7 Kate Rice, "Believe it Or Not, Chores May Be Best Technique," ABC News, 16 February 2010, http://abcnews.go.com/Health/story?id=11825 4&page=2.

8 *Improving the Health of Young Canadians* (Ottawa: Canadian Institute for Health Information, 2005).

9 *Ibid.*

10 The results of an Angus Reid Strategies poll cited by Sarah Boesveld in "Let's talk birds & bees, drugs & alcohol, but not money," *Globe and Mail*, 29 September 2009.

11 Amanda Lenhart, *Teens, Cellphones and Texting* (Washington: Pew Research Center, 2010).

12 Dakshana Bascaramurty, "Teen Plastic," *Globe and Mail*, 7 December 2010.

13 John Bowe, "The Copyright Enforcers," *New York Times Magazine*, 8 August 2010.

14 *Ibid.*

15 Beginning in 1999 Napster allowed users to illegally share music online, and at its height had some seventy million users. A legal battle launched in 2002 resulted in its bankruptcy and it subsequently reopened as a legal online music store.

16 In 2010, Limewire, a peer-to-peer file-sharing service, was found guilty of copyright infringement by a U.S. Federal Court.

17 Matt Mason, *The Pirate's Dilemma* (New York: Free Press, 2008), 101.

18 Howard Gardner, *Five Minds for the Future* (Boston: Harvard Business Press, 2008), xiv. The other minds are the disciplined mind, the synthesizing mind, the creating mind and the respectful mind.

19 "Teens Take Stand on Bullying, But Resources Are Still Needed," Harris Polls of teens aged thirteen to eighteen, surveyed online between 14 and 20 April 2010, http://www.harrisinteractive.com/NewsRoom/HarrisPolls/tabid/447/ctl/ReadCustom%20Default/mid/1508/ArticleId/565/Default.aspx.

20 Barbara Coloroso, *The Bully, the Bullied, and the Bystander* (New York: HarperCollins, 2008), 20.

21 Miguel Helft, "Friending the World," *New York Times*, 8 July 2010.

22 See http://www.rotary.org/en/StudentsAndYouth/YouthPrograms/RotaryYouthExchange/Pages/ridefault.aspx for more information.

23 Gardner, *Five Minds for the Future*, xiv.

24 Children's International Summer Villages (www.cisv.org) is a fifty-year-old volunteer organization promoting cross-cultural friendship.

THE TEEN BODY

1   Alissa Quart, *Branded: The Buying and Selling of Teenagers* (New York: Basic Books, 2003), 119.
2   *Ibid.*, 130.
3   David Rider, "Under the needle," *Toronto Star*, 7 July 2006.
4   Letter to the Editor, *Toronto Star*, 13 October 2010.
5   Unnati Gandhi, "Alarm raised on teen alcohol abuse," *Globe and Mail*, 25 October 2006.
6   Kurt Kleiner, "Do You Drink Too Much?", www.magazine.utoronto.ca, Autumn 2010.
7   Quart, *Branded: The Buying and Selling of Teenager*, 137.
8   Dakshana Bascaramurty "Teen hearing loss up 30 per cent," *Globe and Mail*, 18 August 2010.
9   Martin Mittelstaedt, "Cellphones and Cancer," *Globe and Mail*, 25 September 2010.
10 Available at http://www.youtube.com/watch?v=4vqLPvEvkiI.
11 Canadian National Longitudinal Study of Children and Youth, available on the Statistics Canada website at http://www.statcan.gc.ca/cgi-bin/imdb/p2SV.pl?Function=getSurvey&SDDS=4450&lang=en&db=IMDB&dbg=f&adm=8&dis=2.
12 Megan Ogilvie, "Kids don't outgrow puppy fat: Study," *Toronto Star*, 12 May 2006.
13 Jill Mahoney, "Wired teen's latest fix: a jolt of java," *Globe and Mail*, 28 October 2006.
14 Tralee Pearce, "Diabetes app designed with teen behaviour in mind," *Globe and Mail*, 27 December 2010.

THE TEEN-PARENT CONNECTION

1   If you're feeling uncomfortable texting, ask your teen for a quick introduction, and if you're confused by the abbreviations that young people use you can practise on www.lingo2word.com. This website offers a service that works both ways—it can translate that text lingo you received into plain English or turn your own message into text short form ready to send.

2 Jan Hoffman, "The Guilt-Trip Casserole," *New York Times*, 4 October 2009.

3 See http://www.commonsensemedia.org/expert-interview-constance-steinkuehler.

4 Summarized from the *Thirteen* (2003) DVD cast discussion.

5 Neufeld and Maté, *Hold On to Your Kids*, 184.

6 See http://parentingteens.about.com/cs/disciplin1/a/curfewtips.htm.

7 Lenhart, *Teens, Cellphones and Texting*.

8 At time of writing, the fee for downloading the contract was $10.

9 See http://www.youtube.com/watch?v=Z2mf8DtWWd8&playnext-1&list-PL2AACB3B8A43D8B3B.

10 Rachel Simmons, *Odd Girl Out* (New York: Harcourt, Inc. 2002), 214.

11 Barbara Kingsolver, "Letter to a Daughter at Thirteen" in Faith Conlon and Gail Hudson, eds., *I Wanna Be Sedated* (Emeryville, CA: Seal Press, 2005), 31.

12 Rising from 22 percent in April 2009 to 42 percent in May 2010. Pew Internet and American Life Project survey, 7 September 2010.

13 According to a survey conducted by Ipsos Reid and Microsoft reported in *Backbone*, September 2010, 6.

14 Gardner, *Five Minds for the Future*, xiii.

15 Brooks Barnes, "Forget Shhh! Theaters Want You to Sing Along," *New York Times*, 12 July 2010.

16 Anne Frank, *Anne Frank: The Diary of a Young Girl* (New York: Pocket Books, 1958), 235.

17 Stephen J. Lyons, "Commuting with Rose" in *I Wanna be Sedated*, 245.

18 Brizendine, *The Female Brain*, 52.

19 Vanier, *Becoming Human*, 9.

20 Rohini B. Ramanathan, "Parent as Riverbank!", 8 July 2005 at http://rohini-ramanathan.sulekha.com/blog/post/2005/07/parent-as-riverbank.htm (accessed 17 March 2011).

CONCLUSION

1   *Anne Frank: The Diary of a Young Girl*, 234.
2   Valerie Grove, *The Compleat Woman* (London: The Hogarth Press, 1988), 113.